14-2662-3   (1-17-68)

ESSAYS BY DIVERS HANDS

BEING THE

TRANSACTIONS

OF THE

ROYAL SOCIETY OF LITERATURE
OF THE UNITED KINGDOM

NEW SERIES

VOL. XVIII

EDITED BY St. JOHN ERVINE, LL.D., F.R.S.L.

MEMBER OF THE IRISH ACADEMY

LONDON:

HUMPHREY MILFORD

OXFORD UNIVERSITY PRESS

———

MCMXL

Made and printed in Great Britain by
Adlard & Son, Ltd.,
at their works, Bartholomew Press, Dorking.

CONTENTS.

INTRODUCTION.

By St. John Ervine, LL.D., Member of the Irish
Academy, F.R.S.L.

The papers assembled in this volume are unusually
varied in subject, even for a collection of Essays by
Divers Hands. They range from Mr. Lawrence
Tanner's report of literary links with Westminster
Abbey in the seventeenth and eighteenth centuries to
Mr. A. Yusuf Ali's account of an Indian poet, Iqbal,
who died in 1939, and they include two Tredegar
Memorial Lectures instead of one. Had the times
been normal, Mr. Michael Roberts's lecture on 'The
Dignity of English Thought' would have appeared
in the succeeding volume to this, but as none of us
knows how far publication of anything will be possible
a year hence, it has been thought advisable to publish
it now, lest the succeeding volume should have to
be deferred a long time. Mr. Hardy Wallis's 'Fugitive
Poetry' and Dr. Robin Flower's erudite paper on
'Lost Manuscripts' will fascinate the reader to whom
all the curiosities of literature appeal.

But although the essays are exceptionally diverse
in theme, a connecting link is detectable in at least
four of them : the two Tredegar Memorial Lectures,
Mr. Ali's 'Doctrine of Human Personality in Iqbal's
Poetry,' and Dr. Percy Spielmann's consideration of

'The Effect of Scientific Thought on the Arts and Literature.' There is in each of them some concern with the recurring inquiry, "What is Truth?" which has long been regarded as a jest by Pilate, though there is nothing in St. John's Gospel, where alone it is reported, to show that Pilate was not perfectly serious when he said it. Each of them, too, concerns itself with the equally recurrent question, How may Truth best be stated? There is no discredit to the authors of the essays in the fact that they leave us where we were. Where else, indeed, could they have left us? "A normally-constituted truth," Dr. Stockman says in Ibsen's play, 'An Enemy of the People,' "lives . . . seventeen or eighteen years; at the outside, twenty; very seldom more. And truths so patriarchal as that are always shockingly emaciated; yet it's not till then that the majority takes them up and recommends them to society as wholesome food." Truth is then, he goes on to say, "like rancid, mouldy ham, producing all the moral scurvy that devastates society." This assertion, if it be true, is disturbing, and may cause us to think that Pilate would have done well to jest when he uttered his rhetorical inquiry. Is truth not perdurable? Had we better abandon all hope of ever finding it? May we not expect to find enough of it to last us for our lifetime? If the quest for truth is futile, then the poet, too, is futile. That fact is sufficient to make it certain that no poet will acknowledge the futility of the search. The most he will admit is that there are two truths, one, local, the other, eternal; and he will insist on our duty to try to distinguish between the two. He may confess

that although a man may recognize local truth, even
if, as Dr. Stockmann asserts, he seldom sees it until
it begins to smell, he can scarcely expect to recognize
eternal truth. What *that* is, God only knows.

Here, then, we are involved in the old problem,
and our essayists attempt, as best they can, to cope
with it. The superstition of our time, that wisdom
is to be found only in the mind of youth, seems to
have possessed the thoughts of Iqbal, who, Mr. A.
Yusuf Ali tells us, believed that Western Civilization
was dying, a belief he derived chiefly, it transpires,
from a perusal of Spengler's superficial work, ' Decline
of the West.' This view, Mr. Ali continues, expressed
" the general sentiment of the rising generation in
India," and Iqbal confirmed himself in his own belief
by listening to the applause of immaturity. This is
a habit no less Occidental than Oriental : we all
mistake applause for proof, and are inclined to think
well of those who share our opinions. But of all the
cant which has afflicted the mind of man, none is at
once so puerile and dangerously delusive as that which
asserts the profound wisdom of the young and pro-
claims the supreme sanctity of callow thought. The
regimented youth depends, in the last resort, on the
guidance of an admired elder, and is too prone,
because of his lack of education, to take his instruction from mumbo-jumbo men with magic wands and
high vocal velocity. The spectacle of adolescents
imagining that they are forming minds when they are
merely forming fours is extremely discouraging. It
becomes dangerous when the drilled boys and girls
attempt to enforce their drill-book opinions. Goose-
stepping intellects are, no doubt, advantageous to

dictators, but can we comfortably contemplate a world inhabited by myriads of minds with but a single thought ?   The Dean, in Ibsen's play, attempts to comfort Brand by telling him that " men need a rule in all they do."

> " Each order'd mode of life proclaims
> One Law, that goes by many names.
> The Artist calls it School, and I'm
> Mistaken if I have not heard
> Our soldiers call it keeping time.
> Ah, yes, friend that's the very word !
> That's what the State desires at last !
> Double-quick time gets on too fast,
> And goose-step lags too far behind ;
> All men to step alike, and beat
> The selfsame music with their feet,
> That is the method to its mind."

It was this method which filled the thoughts of the French Minister of Education with awe and wonder when he reflected that at any given moment every child in France would be repeating the same lesson. But that prospect delights not Brand, who, having heard the Dean with impatience, exclaims, in condemnation of such a state of life :

> " Kennel the eagle ;—and let loose
> On empyrean flights, the goose."

The Dean's argument is not demolished by Brand's heroic cry.   He has a case.   Confusion, he reminds Brand, came on mankind at the Tower of Babel when many kinds of speech replaced a universal language ; a confusion wrought deliberately by Omniscience, according to the Book of Genesis, lest man should become imaginatively omnipotent. Those who defy the world, he declares, are "death-doom'd."

> "When God desires a man to fall,
> He makes him an Original."

Is there any way of escape from the horns of this dilemma? If there is, we have not found it, and perhaps its discovery is not desirable. Dr. Johnson may have been right when he suggested to Boswell that man must be martyred for truth's sake. The swing of the pendulum from left to right and back again enables us to tell the time. If the pendulum were perfectly poised, the clock would stop. It should be enough for us that our perceptions are different, and that no man's vision is utterly reject-able. If three men, one with long sight, another with normal sight, and the third with short sight, cross the desert together, the first will see the hills and oasis long before the others. How unreasonable would be the short-sighted man, if, having heard his long-sighted comrade exclaim that the goal is ahead, he should reply petulantly, "I can't see it, and I always say, 'seeing's believing.'" We can only get along if we pool our resources and use each other's lines of communication.

Mr. Richard Church, in his lecture, remarks on the poet's perception, as he grows older, of the need of a means of communication with the crowd. "A poet," he says, "cannot fully release his genius until he feels that he is expressing himself through a medium which is likely to be understood and accepted by the audience at which he is aiming." And he pleads with the poet to modify the severity of his style,

at all events, in the medium of the novel, so that he
may be understood. The plea is timely in an age of
self-consciously proletarian poets of the upper middle
class, many of whom fail to perceive the difference
between poetry and political propaganda. These
poets are almost invariably incomprehensible to the
people whom they seek to placate. Nor is it the
proletariat alone which is bewildered and repelled
by their profuse strains of over-premeditated art.
Educated men and women feel no less confounded
when they read verse which suggests that the Muses
have taken to drink. Here, indeed, is a paradox.
The poet, seeking to conciliate the common man,
succeeds only in alienating him. Shakespeare did
not disguise his aversion from the rude mechanicals
who uttered such a deal of stinking breath, yet he
has survived for several centuries in the regard even
of the class he despised ; but our public school and
university proletarian poets, shamelessly flattering
the crowd in their obscure stanzas, fail to find readers
outside the small circles of expensive intellectuals
who advocate communism on increment which is
largely unearned. Our sympathy with Mr. Church's
plea need not delude us into supposing that the poet
must neglect his style to be understood. How high a
price are we prepared to pay for comprehension ? No
price, according to Dr. Stockmann, can be too high
for truth. " What does it matter," he exclaimed
at that meeting of his fellow townsmen in Captain
Horster's house, " if a lying community is ruined !
Let it be levelled to the ground, say I ! All men who
live upon a lie ought to be exterminated like vermin !
You'll end by poisoning the whole country ; you'll

bring it to such a pass that the whole country will deserve to perish. And if ever it comes to that, I shall say with my whole heart : Perish the country ! Perish all its people ! " But not, we may presume, Perish Dr. Stockmann ! If the people are to believe as Dr. Stockmann believes or perish, how are they to satisfy themselves that Dr. Stockmann is right ? The people, all but eight of them, perished, we are informed by the Pentateuch, but when the Ark was beached again, and Noah and his children stepped on to dry land, they begot a race which seemed not to be much of an improvement, if it was any improvement at all, on the race which had been drowned. Mr. Church, rightly desirous of a means of communication, omits to consider one problem. Are we to establish contact with the crowd by reducing ourselves to the lowest level, or to establish it by raising the crowd to a higher level ? The Book of Common Prayer, we were recently told, is not understood of the people, and it must, therefore, be rendered more colloquial. What, exclaim those who are more literary than religious, are we to debase good speech ! Why not raise the people to its level instead of reducing it to theirs ? We forget, do we not, that the function of language is to make thought understandable ? If it is kept in archaic clothes, it renders thought incomprehensible and, therefore, useless.

Dr. Spielmann gives us timely warning of the devastation that may be wrought in an artist's mind by ill-considered science. We have seen how the belief that we are the creatures of our environment sterilized John Galsworthy's characters, and may note at this moment the ruinous effect on writing

of Drs. Freud and Jung. " The main underlying
cause of the abandonment of tradition," says Dr.
Spielmann, " is that current art of any branch, to be
honest, must be a reflection of the life of the time."
If it is no more than that, it is merely journalism,
surpassing or falling below the level of the daily paper
only in so far as it is good or bad journalism. A
reflection disappears when the thing reflected has
ceased to exist. If art is only a picture of transient
actuality, there is no art. The reflection, if it can
be fixed, is not any more interesting than a solved
crossword puzzle or an old newspaper account of a
brawl which was settled long ago. It may be true,
as Dr. Spielmann asserts, though I think he exagge-
rates, " that the hideosities of steel and concrete that
are allowed to mar our country-side, do more nearly
represent the state of society to-day " than the
" Queen Anne and Georgian architecture " with which
we feel at peace as we admire it ; but what shall we
do with these " hideosities " when we have recovered
our nerve and are no longer upset by violent emotions?
They will not " represent " our state of society and,
since they offer us neither peace nor occasion for
admiration, will then afflict us. Shall we demolish
them ? Are we to create only those things which reflect
the momentary mood, destroying them when they
have ceased to reflect it ? This, surely, is far from
the poet's purpose, which is, so far as he can compass
it, with permanence. I may bemuse myself with the
desire to portray the thing as I see it, but there is
still the thing as it is. Ought we not to try to show
it as it is ? A gin-sodden portrait-painter may
see all men as drunkards, and paint them with

grog-blossomed faces, but all men are not drunkards, and the painter who portrays them as such deceives himself and us. The truth is not in him.

We must not, however, delude ourselves with the belief that the sole business of the artist is to reproduce reality, that there is nothing to reproduce but the thing itself. If that were true, and there were a thing itself, evident, defined and generally perceived, there would not be any argument or dispute about it. It would be precisely the same to every eye, and any portrait of a man at a particular moment of his life would be like all the portraits of him at that period. This, as Dr. Spielmann says, will not do for us. We must vary from type even if we have to break the type to do so. We recognize that there is not only the thing itself, but my view of it, and your view of it : three views so dissimilar that they may not be identifiable as views of the same thing. And there is also our belief about what the thing ought to be. How is the artist to cope with these varieties of the thing so that he may produce a thing that is recognizable, recognizable, too, by the largest number of persons. For it is a vain superstition to suppose that he works only for his own pleasure. If he has no wish to gratify anybody but himself, why does he take so much trouble to call attention to his work ? Why paint at all, when he need only imagine his subject ?

It is this confusion of purposes which causes so much confusion of mind among artists, so much tub-thumping, so much circus-work and drumming. What a strange argument it is, for example, that " the reproduction of art along accepted lines has been worked out, and no possibility remains for original work—everything now is more or less a copy of everything else, because it has been done before. . . . Who, to-day, can paint flowers as well as the Seventeenth Century Dutch ? " Here, surely, is some misunderstanding of life itself. Spring performs its delicate miracle every year. Are we to conclude that the reproduction of primroses is pure waste of time since we have no reason to suppose that this spring's blossoms are better than last spring's ? If we cannot paint flowers better than they were painted by the Seventeenth Century Dutch, then, perhaps, we had better not paint them at all, but are we certain that we cannot ? And even if it be true that we are less competent in this style than these Dutch, are we to cease painting flowers to look like flowers and begin to paint them to look like steel rods or lumps of broken concrete ? The heresy of our time is that by resolving bodies into their elements, we perceive the bodies more clearly ; as if the beauty of a figure were made more apparent by dissection ! Morbid addiction to metaphysics ends in such aimless adventures as those mentioned by Dr. Spielmann, when alchemists expended their energies in a fruitless effort to separate the properties of matter from matter itself. How could such a separation be made ? Without matter, there are no properties of matter.

Mr. Michael Roberts, in his most interesting lecture, ' The Dignity of English Thought,' is more divided in his allegiance than he, perhaps, perceives. Superficially, he seems over-concerned about transitions and preoccupied with the need of adapting oneself to one's environment, when he had much better be

concerned with the need of adapting one's environment to oneself; but he does not forget that the
poet is intensely individual, intensely an aristocrat,
and the most certain of all men to be the victim of the
dictating proletariat. A citizen, in 'Julius Caesar,'
desired to have Cinna, the poet, torn to pieces for
his bad verses. If we could feel assured that the mob,
especially when it is in a riotous mood, would tear
to pieces only bad poets, we might well admire the
mob, but is it not more likely to destroy the good
poet and put laurels on the bad ? The elder Mill felt
assured that men had only to be educated to become
good and wise. Put a primer in the child's hands—
and behold a mixture of Solomon and Socrates,
wearing the white flower of a blameless life. The
hope has proved to be delusive. Seventy years of
free and compulsory education are not enough in
which to produce a fine race, and we may be pardoned
if, looking at some of our compulsorily and freely
instructed people, we wonder whether any number of
years will be enough. The general mind is even
shallower than it was in days when instruction was
less widely dispersed; for men, in times when they
did their own thinking, such as it was, had greater
tenacity of thought than is possessed to-day by those
who have their thinking done for them by the B.B.C.
and the public press. Within a week of the sinking
of the " Graf Spee," a young soldier in France, during
a broadcast, confessed that he had not the faintest
notion of the names of the ships that sent her hurrying
into Montevideo. His ignorance is not, perhaps,
important, but it signifies an extraordinary detachment from events which is more likely to be the result

of intellectual lassitude than of philosophy.   We may
yet find that men know nothing because we teach
them too much.

It is evident, then, from these essays, diverse and
detached from each other though they seem to be,
that we are still deeply perturbed about the destiny
of man.   We are flurried between two ways of
thought : one which obliges us to submerge our own
personalities in the general good of the community ;
another which urges us to assert ourselves whatever
happens.   The Dean may have been right when he
told Brand to stick to a rule and avoid originality,
but it is crystal clear that if we do, there will soon
be an end of us.   There is no development without
discontent, nor any growth without aspiration.   We
may have to kill the rebel, but we shall die if we
prevent his birth.

THE TREDEGAR MEMORIAL LECTURE FOR 1938.

The Tredegar Lecture perpetuates the honoured memory of the first Viscount Tredegar of the second creation. It was founded in 1935 by his son, the second Viscount, a Fellow of this Society since 1928.

THE POET AND THE NOVEL.

By Richard Church.

[Read October 12th, 1938.]

THROUGHOUT the nineteenth century, and increasingly so during the present century, the cultivation of the novel—the writing of it, and the reading of it— has tended to become separated from all idea of literary consciousness and even general culture. That state of letters has become so marked that young poets, setting out on their great careers, have looked on the novel with abhorrence, and upon novelists as mere tradesmen. It is a pretty piece of snobbery ; but it is symptomatic, and it follows upon fact. And the fact is that the novel has fallen upon evil days.

I want first to discover with you the main necessities of the poet's development. That development follows roughly the same lines as the development of every other man or woman. We all begin our *real* life, that is to say, our *conscious* or *seeking* life, enveloped in those clouds of glory of which the poet Wordsworth has sung. Heaven lies about us in our infancy ; and it is a state of affairs making for isolation. All that we see is an estate which we, as individuals, have just inherited. We stand, as it were, on the threshold of life ; and the building before us is a vast hall of mirrors. As soon as we take one step forward, into the range of consciousness, those mirrors re-create us, and the world is crowded with our own ego.

It is most exciting and inspiriting—until something happens. Some derisive outside force, an intangible power which we may call Time, or Experience, or, if we are up to date and good Marxists, Economic Pressure, flicks a heel and cracks one, only *one*, mind you, of those mirrors ; and suddenly the whole universe goes wrong. Our subjects, that were so beautiful, so perfect a replica of ourselves, are cracked and warped, and our flawless consciousness of self is no longer flawless.

If we are brave, we step forward to examine the phenomenon. If we are still childish and afraid, we step backward. But whatever way we step, we find ourselves no longer isolated. We are in a crowd ; but now an *unfamiliar* crowd ; and every individual in that crowd has suffered an experience—a devastating experience—similar to our own. From that moment we begin to live. From that moment we begin to move from self-consciousness to *true* consciousness.

In this rather fanciful picture, I have drawn your attention to the two states of development in which every intelligent man and woman finds himself and herself. It is an inevitable process, a metabolism from which none of us can escape, except by arresting our development, by slipping into insanity, by sidetracking ourselves into anti-social conditions either pathological or criminal.

In that first state, the " cloud of glory " period, when we are alone and superb in the universe, we have nothing to express except ourselves, and our few primitive reactions as we examine, with wonder and wild excitement, the estate which we have just inherited. It is, therefore, a period of lyrical expression. The poet writes his most eloquent, his most ecstatic verse at this period of his life. I won't say his most rhythmic or his best. That is another matter, involving discussion that would lead us away from what we have in hand to-day.

But there it is. The youngster lit up with glory. Singing like a lark just before daybreak ; his voice a little tremulous, dewy, fearful. But the cadences come pouring out, without thought or afterthought. Certainly no afterthought. The poet is not yet a Prometheus, chained to the rock, with vultures gnawing at his vitals. No ; he is free, because he is not in contact with his fellow men. He doesn't know they exist. He is a sort of Robinson Crusoe, after the shipwreck which we call birth. He is monarch of all he surveys. And he sings about it. That is the age of lyricism ; a glorious age, one which we look back on with nostalgia, although we pretend to be a little contemptuous of it, of its pretensions, its ignorance, its crass *naïveté*.

And when that is over, the poet discovers—and this is one of the most marked signs of maturity— that he is a social animal. What is the result ? We all know the result ; for we all have the experience. We lose ourselves, and in that loss truly discover

ourselves.   It is one of the most impressive paradoxes
of the many which punctuate our life-story.

And how does it affect the poet's work ?   It begins
by abating his lyrical fervour.   If often silences him
for a time, because the old ego from which his music
sprang is cancelled out.   He is crushed, disillusioned.
He is only one of the many ;   only a cog in the wheel
of society.

But after this sense of defeat has worn off, he wakes
up again to a new exhilaration.   He finds delight once
more ;   but this time it is an *impersonal* delight.   He
develops a sense of character, and begins to study the
conflict of character.   His old ecstasies are now
focused down from cosmic things to human things,
and to the drama of man with man.   He introduces a
new, and a stiffer ingredient into his work.   We may
call it ethics ;   or if it takes a more dogmatic turn, we
may call it politics.   But whatever it is, and in whatever degree of intensity it affects him, it is always
compounded of the one element ;   and that element
is the conduct of man with man.

The poet may have retained his lyrical technique ;
but his adult mind demands something else ;   something formal, something solid, upon which he can
begin to build an expression that is structural, archi-
tectural.

He wants to prove himself in a more responsible
way, with work sustained over the skeleton of a moral
philosophy.   And that philosophy is the growth of
his contact with his fellow creatures.   It has not the
sublime and egotistic simplicity of youth and youth's
lyricism.   It is intricate with humility ;   complicated
with detailed experiences, day-to-day experiences,

which have come to him as a member of human
society, a man amongst men. He has reached the
epic stage, the dramatic stage—one or other of them,
according to his nature. But in both cases he must
have an art-form which is continuous and elaborate.

Where is he to find it to-day ? We know what the
answer is. We know what a pitiful anachronism it
is to see a poet struggling with an epic poem. Even
a century ago our poets had begun to be uneasy about
it. From a historical point of view it is hard to evade
the uncertainty when we ask, Why did Browning
write ' The Ring and the Book ' in blank verse ? It
is still harder to evade it when we think of Bridges'
' Testament of Beauty.' Was there not a touch of
the ivory tower in the attitude of those poets ; a
defeatism which made them pretend not to care if
their audiences should be restricted to the cultured
few ? Or did they think it worth while making that
sacrifice, in order to propitiate posterity, fearing that
to express themselves in prose fiction would be to limit
their chances of survival ? The point is this : that
whatever the chances may be for survival, the poet
must, sooner or later, seek a form of self-expression
that is sustained, and which reflects and contains
the results of his social experience. And he knows
to-day, that if he tries to find that expression in narrative verse, or in verse-drama, he is committing himself to archaism, he is assuming fancy-dress, just as
surely as Edmund Spenser was when he wrote the
' Shepherds' Calender.'

An initial discouragement of this sort is fatal. Self-
consciousness, and a sense of futility in one's medium
—these are the two worst enemies of the creative

mood. They are the cause of much of the confusion and eccentricity shown by poets to-day, even in short, lyrical work. A poet cannot fully release his genius until he feels that he is expressing himself through a medium which is likely to be understood and accepted by the audience at which he is aiming. That is only natural. For a poet, being an artist, knows that his first consideration must be economy ; economy of mood, of statement.

The most directly economical thing a poet can do is to seize upon a medium which he knows is good currency among his contemporaries. That is why he turns to the novel. He sees it is the modern form of the epic poem ; a vast shape, capable of driving him to the fullest stretch of his intellectual muscles. He sees that he will have to put into it all the discipline that he has learned by the practice of verse. He sees that he will have to bring to it all that he has learned from life, and all the great surmises, all the possibilities of order and organization, which are now looming so large in his consciousness, the consciousness of a maturing man.

And what does he find ? To begin with, he finds that he has entered a world which has never heard of him. He may be a well-known poet, with a secure reputation built up by many years of excellent work. Critics will know him, and the small public interested in literature *as* literature will value him. He will get his lyrics printed in the intellectual weeklies and monthlies ; and his publisher will not be unduly depressed when he brings along, from time to time, a new collection of verse. But it has come to this : the poet has decided to write a novel ! He pretends that it is because he wants money, and he puts on the pose of being hard-boiled, slightly cynical, reluctantly driven to this course by a philistinish world.

In his heart, however, he knows this is nonsense. He knows that really he is afraid. And he is afraid of two things. First, he is afraid of the new medium ; the " capital difficulty of prose," as Quiller-Couch calls it, and of the enormous capacity of the novel-form. He feels as I imagine a young architect must feel, who has decided to enter for a competition to submit designs for the building of a great cathedral. To the poet, approaching the problem in his pride of past achievement, the novel *is* a cathedral.

We have to be sympathetic toward the poet at this nervous stage in his career. In a properly ordered world, he ought not to be faced with this problem. He ought to be able to proceed smoothly, in an unimpeded course of psychological growth, from lyric to epic form, carrying his reputation from achievement in the one to achievement in the other. But the world is not properly ordered. One consequence of that universally applicable fact is that when the poet begins as a novelist, he addresses himself to a public that has never heard of him. What is more, he addresses himself to a trade—I refer to the booksellers —that has never heard of him.

He has come up against something for which he was perhaps quite unprepared. There is always a streak of social innocence in the poet's nature. It is probable that when he wrote his first novel, and put into it all the verbal austerity, all the crystallization of form, which he had learned during many years' practice of verse-making, he believed that this artistic consciousness would be at once recognized, appreciated and commended.

He has now learned that the majority of the great fiction-reading public is totally indifferent to his technique, his scrupulous use of words, his passion for cadence in the prose paragraph. And when I say *indifferent*, I am putting it mildly. I ought rather to say *antagonistic, suspicious*. You know that Robert Louis Stevenson was thirty-five years of age before he had any success with his novels. One reason is that his writing was verbally conscious. He used words with exquisite care. He was almost a verbal dandy. And the public think that is showing off. They call it highbrow.

The poet, when he commences novelist, has to learn that his deliberate art is not only unnoticed, but is unwanted. So long as he displays his craft learned as a poet ; the cunning manipulation of vowel and consonant, the harmonies, the pauses ; the etymological niceties that imply all the historical values of the words he uses, so long as he makes a show of that in his prose, the public will suspect him, and will refuse to read him.

Does he have to give up the mechanics of his art ? Does he have to betray himself, and prostitute his skill ? Certainly not. He has to become even more skilful. He has now to learn that last and most difficult lesson of the professional writer. He has to learn to conceal his art. Some great novelists have never learned that. Henry James and Conrad, for example. That is why, for all their fame amongst discriminating people, and their adulation from other writers, they have nevertheless never become universal in their appeal. The translators of the Bible, and Tolstoy, Balzac, John Bunyan, Charles Dickens, all these were writers who concealed their art. Perhaps because their attention was on other things, things extraneous to the form in which they were expressed. Whatever the cause, those writers, and many smaller writers like them, concealed their art. And the result was an immediate relationship with the general public, the public totally indifferent and even inimical to literary perfection.

The poet has to learn that. It is the first step in a new humility. I said that many novelists are concerned with extraneous matters. That is important, for it advances another factor of obscuration in the relationship between the poet and the public. Hitherto he has been very much concerned with *how* he says a thing; more concerned about that, perhaps, than with *what* he says. It is a privilege of youth, and a privilege of lyricism.

But a new responsibility has come with the maturing mind. The poet is undertaking social inquiry in his work. He is no longer writing about himself. As I said earlier this afternoon, he is now undertaking to write not so much, as Milton said, " To justify the ways of God to men," as to justify the ways of *men* to men, and particularly of " man's *inhumanity* to man." He has to become practical. Which is to say that he has to become a statesman, able to foresee the follies of mankind and of individuals, and to explain them in terms of wisdom and forbearance.

It is a task for the mature mind, and it brings new dangers and difficulties. One of the chief of these dangers is what I should call " losing sight of the wood for the trees." Or you might prefer to call it getting swamped by detail. And that is what has happened to the novel. Not only has it been attacked from below, as I have already shown. It has also been attacked from above.

Here, then, are the two impingements, from above and from below, which magnify the activities of the book-world. Last year some 5000 novels were published in this country. It is a formidable number. Editors, reviewers, librarians and the reading public, they all wilt under the oppression. *Number* is one of the greatest satirists of mankind. You see a pair of lovers walking through a wood, and you have seen something which can inspire the poets and musicians of the world. But if that unit is multiplied, if you see five hundred pairs of lovers walking through the wood, you see something which is a disgusting nightmare, something which can inspire nobody except perhaps one of our latter-day dictators.

Unfortunately, the poet is bad at pushing. He lacks the effrontery. His skin is too thin, and his pride is too great. The sensibility which makes him a poet also makes him a bad thruster. He has been spoiled, too, by living in a little world comparatively civilized, a world preoccupied with niceties of human impulse and of literary technique.

We want to consider now the poet who survives all this, the poet with sufficient dynamic to *command* an audience. We can assume that he has fought his way, and will continue to fight his way, through the crowd of irrelevant rivals, the people who have no instinct for art, and are therefore no rivals at all, but merely a noisy obstruction.

Well, now we see him emerged. He has cleared a space for himself. And what comes next ? The *real* fight comes next. And it is the same fight which he had at first, when he was striving for lyrical expression in verse. It is the authentic battle which all artists wage all their lives, the battle with technique.

And now I must ask your indulgence. For I am struggling to bring to light a something which is intangible. I am struggling to find a definition for *Form in Art*. It is a matter over which there has been argument and warfare between critics and philosophers since the days of Aristotle. One man's form is another man's anarchy. To-day, for example, we recognize the form in Shelley's ' Prometheus Unbound ' and in Thomas Hardy's ' Jude the Obscure.' But when those books were published, quite intelligent critics foamed at the mouth at having to deal with such chaotic and obscene drivel. Conceptions of form alter not only as between individuals, but also with the passage of time and the changes in aesthetic fashion.

The trouble is, moreover, that this matter is an essential one, upon which the critic must found his final judgment of a writer's work. Form is the direct expression of a writer's character, as it is shaped by his experience. It is the direct index of his maturity. According to its command in a work of art, so are we able to judge how adequately has the author learned to command the realities of history, the pro-portions both of his own experience and of the larger experiences of humanity, brought to him through the proxy of his imagination.

It is this experience, this maturing of mind, which urge the poet to seek a medium of expression wherewith he can lay out what he has acquired. I have already shown why he is forced to turn to the novel for this. The novel is now his adequate vehicle. And you have to remember this, that no artist is himself, is capable of full and free expression and achievement, if he is constrained to a vehicle either that he has outgrown, or that he is not yet in control of. Without that fitness between the workman and his material, perfect achievement, the great work of art, cannot result. And what is this greatness ?

We will first find it in a little thing, and to do so I will quote a passage from an essay by the poet Lascelles Abercrombie. This is what he says : " Though we may agree that greatness in poetry strictly belongs to form, we must make out more exactly what it means. In any noticeable moment of poetry, we see that there is a certain set of words responsible for it. But when, at the end of a poem, we receive its final impression as a whole, there is no set of words that is directly responsible for that. It certainly comes to us as the result of *all* the words in the poem, but not *directly*. It is the organized accumulation of the whole series of momentary impressions : the impression made by all the other impressions united together. Often enough the series of impressions is so short, and accumulates into a self-sufficient whole so rapidly and simply, that the process is not noticed at all. The whole poem seems to form a single moment, and may legitimately be so described ; and we seem to take its completed impression directly from the words. Here is a poem

of Allingham's which is, perhaps, as simple an instance
of the art of poetry as we could have :

> ' Four ducks on a pond,
> A grass bank beyond,
> A blue sky of Spring,
> White clouds on the wing :
> What a little thing
> To remember for years—
> To remember with tears.' "

I have chosen the passage because of its clarity,
and also because the poem exemplifying it is one of
the most direct and simple in the English language.
You all know the poem. Now I want to ask you to
consider its form, the growth of memory from a
picture, the transmutation of memory to a state of
emotional poignancy that reacts upon the picture,
and so the completion of a circle of evocatory beauty.
Note that process in miniature. Now compare it to
the process involved in the building of two of the
longest prose fictions written during this century. I
refer to Proust's prose-epic so brilliantly translated
by Scott-Moncrieff, and to Dorothy Richardson's
twelve-volume life-work which has been appearing
during the last twenty-five years under the title of
' Pilgrimage.'

Now comes the revealing discovery. Those two
prose works, each filling a structure demanding
hundreds of thousands of words, are based upon the
same form as that poem of seven lines.

If that is so, you might ask me what need the poet
has to depart from the lyrical mood ? If the same

form can be found in a seven-line poem as in a twelve-volume prose fiction, what is all this argument about ? The answer is a complicated one. It takes us back to our earlier consideration of Number ; and to the contrast of the fruits of intuition with the fruits of experience. I will say that the poet has the same need to leave the lyric for the prose fiction as the seed has to burst its husk, to throw up a shoot, to exfoliate and flower, and seed again. The whole process, a shapely and, I would emphasize, a *formal* one, is inherent in that seed, that counterpart of the lyric.

And why must the poet burst out from that first conciseness ? For this reason. You will have noted that the form of Allingham's poem is described by Lascelles Abercrombie as " the organized accumulation of the whole series of *momentary* impressions." He gives further point to that word *momentary* by saying, " Often enough the series of impressions is so short, and accumulates into a self-sufficient whole so rapidly and simply, that the process is not noticed at all."

Now that touches the heart of the matter. It explains why, as I said earlier in this lecture, the poet comes to a time when he feels that direct lyrical expression is too external a process, too much a fleeting thing of chance, coming and going so swiftly that it cannot be seized, or counted upon to return, or examined and sealed with the stamp of his own personality.

Now I referred once more to the strange alchemy of Number. The point is this : that the accumulation of lyrical, of momentary impressions, comes to

more than the sum of those impressions. We do not
live by arithmetic ; we live by a bio-chemical process,
and by something even more irrational than that.
Things stored in our minds acquire properties and
values which they did not possess when we first put
them into stock. It is the same with wine. Wine
changes in the cellar. Some of it becomes food for
the gods ; some of it becomes vinegar. So the poet
never knows quite what he is worth. It is an uneasy
condition to be in. It makes a man feel dishonest.
He must strive to get his vintage of experiences
organized.

I won't follow up this pretty little simile too far.
It has served to illustrate the vitality of *momentary*
impressions, and how that in their vitality they
continue to fecundate. From *momentary* impressions
they develop into *reflective* impressions, and thence
into ideas, or *significant* impressions. And at this
point they are very powerful little atoms, bombinat-
ing about within the original confines of their lyrical
origins, and finally demanding a larger expression
that shall be able to convey not only their first
spontaneity, but also their subsequent significance.
What was lyrical, in short, must now also be philosophical.

That is what Aristotle meant when he said that
Poetry is the most philosophic of all writing. He
took a larger and more complete view of the poet's
function than Plato did. You remember that Plato
would exclude the poet from his ideal commonwealth,
as a disruptive element in society. But that view is
limited to the early, the rebellious, the lyrical phase
of the poet's development.

Aristotle saw that the poet grows, putting his lyrical insight to the service of the community. That is to say, he becomes socially conscious, interested in dramatic values, epic values. It is in this phase of his growth that he turns to the novel. Let us look at him at this moment as Wordsworth sees him. Wordsworth's opinion is valuable, because he was a great poet, a poet in the same kind as Dante ; but he suffered from the difficulty which it is the whole purpose of my lecture to examine. He could not find a medium consonant with his mature spirit. In his ripe years he wrote ' The Excursion.' Now ' The Excursion ' has been cursed and pulled to pieces. Nobody has ever noted that it is rich with the materials from which the greatest novels are made : the swift delineation of character ; a penetrating psychological insight ; a passionate evocation of scene and situation. But let us hear Wordworth's definition of the poet : " He is a man speaking to men : a man, it is true, endowed with more lively sensibility, more enthusiasm and tenderness, who has a greater knowledge of human nature, and a more comprehensive soul, than are supposed to be common among mankind ; a man pleased with his own passions and volitions, and who rejoices more than other men in the spirit of life that is in him, delighting to contemplate similar volitions and passions as manifested in the goings-on of the Universe, and habitually impelled to create them where he does not find them." That is a compre- hensive picture of the poet in his maturity. Words- worth goes on to say, " What then *does* the poet ? He considers man and the objects that surround him as acting and reacting upon each other, so as to produce an infinite complexity of pain and pleasure, he considers man in his own nature and in his ordinary life as contemplating this with a certain quantity of immediate knowledge, with certain convictions, intuitions, and deductions which from habit acquire the quality of intuitions ; he considers him as looking upon this complex scene of ideas and sensations, and finding everywhere objects that immediately excite in him sympathies which, from the necessities of his nature, are accompanied by an over-balance of enjoyment."

That is a great and a mature poet, describing the function of a mature poet. And isn't that function at once recognizable, as the function of a novelist ? If we examine, for example, the process of composition of two of the most perfectly made novels written in English during the last century, we shall find that in every respect, both in the comedic vision of Meredith's ' The Egoist ' and in the tragic vision of Hardy's ' The Woodlanders,' this function of the poet, as laid down by Wordsworth, is carried out to the full.

I have spoken about Hardy's lovely novel ' The Woodlanders.' It is a green book, a sylvan book. Its poignant story, of love and renunciation, is worked out in an atmosphere of cool shades and mossy recesses. It is a book about shyness and the penalties which shy people, shy animals, shy flowers, have to pay in a world which evolves by savagery and blood-lust. That is the central idea of this book. For all great works of art have a central mood or idea. The indecisions of Grace Fitzspiers, by reason of her temperament and her social predicament ; and the indecisions of Giles Winterbourne, by reason of his timid and gentle character; these bring about the climax and the exquisite tragedy of the tale.

And now listen to the same drama in a nutshell. It is contained in a short lyric written by Hardy, probably at a distance of many years from the period when he wrote the novel. But it is the same mood, the same story, and you will notice, finally, that it has *the same form:*

> " I say, ' I'll seek her side
> Ere hindrance interposes,'
> But eve in midnight closes,
> And here I still abide.

> " When darkness wears I see
> Her sad eyes in a vision,
> They ask, ' What indecision
> Detains you, Love, from me ?

> " The creaking Hinge is oiled,
> I have unbarred the backway,
> But you tread not the trackway ;
> And shall the thing be spoiled ?

> " Far cockcrows echo shrill,
> The shadows are abating,
> And I am waiting, waiting ;
> But O, you tarry still ! ' "

SOME LITERARY LINKS WITH WESTMINSTER ABBEY.

By Lawrence E. Tanner, M.V.O., F.S.A.

(Keeper of the Library and Muniments, Westminster Abbey.)

[Read February 15th, 1939.]

In a well-known passage in Boswell's ' Johnson ' he records that Dr. Johnson, speaking of Goldsmith, remarked "I remember once being with Goldsmith in Westminster Abbey. While we surveyed the Poets' Corner I said to him,

" Forsitan et nostrum nomen miscebitur istis."

When we got to Temple Bar he stopped me, pointed to the heads upon it, and slily whispered me,

" Forsitan et nostrum nomen miscebitur *istis.*"*

I quote this story because I propose this evening to speak not so much—or only incidentally—of those who rest in Poets' Corner as of some of those poets, writers and men of letters who were connected during their lives in one way or another with the Abbey and its Precincts, one of whom, at least, was to suffer the fate suggested by Goldsmith.

I propose, further, to limit myself mostly to the seventeenth and eighteenth centuries, and although

* Boswell's 'Johnson,' ed. Birkbeck Hill, vol. ii, 238 (April 30th, 1773).

in what I have to say there may not be anything particularly new, yet I hope that it may be possible to glean from our records at the Abbey and from other sources some few stray facts which may be of interest and may, perhaps, help to illustrate the lives of those of whom I shall speak.

At the beginning of our period the Dean of Westminster was the aged Dr. Gabriel Goodman, " a right good man indeed," as he was described, "of singular integrity and an especial patron of literature."* He had been appointed as far back as 1561, and he was to die on June 17th, 1601, some two years before the Sovereign with whose reign his own had been almost coincident. He was a lover of peace and moderation, and he had—as he put it—" agreed very brotherly with great quietness " with his Chapter and was secure in their affection and support. But above all he was a Welshman, and that was no bad thing to be when a Tudor ruled the land. The highroad from Wales to London was well-trodden in the sixteenth century, and particularly that portion of it which turned aside to the Deanery of Westminster while Dr. Goodman reigned supreme. Indeed among our Muniments there has been preserved a letter from an anxious Welsh father to his son, whom the Dean had taken into his household, which contains the sensible warning, " peest not yʳ Maysters house wᵗʰ straungers of yʳ country but as litle as you can," while among the treasures of the Library is a copy of the great folio Bible translated for the first time into Welsh, presented in 1588 by the translator, Wm. Morgan, afterwards Bishop of St. Asaph, who had

* Howel, ' Londinopolis ' (1657), p. 354.

stayed with the Dean in order to see it through the Press.

It was no doubt the Welsh influence which brought two brothers from the borders of Wales to Westminster School early in Goodman's reign. The younger, Richard Hakluyt, was to attain fame as the Father of English Geography, and to return to Westminster as a Prebendary a year after Goodman's death. He became a Queen's Scholar at Westminster in 1564. In the dedication to Sir Francis Walsingham of his *magnum opus*, ' The Principall Navigations . . . of the English Nation ' he tells us :

" I do remember that being a youth, and one of her Majesties scholars at Westminster that fruitfull nurserie, it was my happe to visit the chamber of M. *Richard Hakluyt* my cosin, a Gentleman of the Middle Temple, when I found lying open vpon his boord certeine bookes of Cosmographie, with an vniuersall Mappe : he seeing me somewhat curious in the view thereof, began to instruct my ignorance, by shewing me the diuision of the earth into three parts after the olde account, and then according to the latter, & better distribution, into more : he pointed with his wand to all the knowen Seas, Gulfs, Bayes, Straights, Capes, Riuers, Empires, Kingdomes, Dukedomes, and Territories of ech part, with declaration also of their speciall commodities, & particular wants, which by the benefit of traffike, & entercourse of merchants, are plentifully supplied.   From the Mappe he brought me to the Bible, and turning to the 107 Psalme, directed mee to the 23 & 24 verses, where I read, that they which go downe to the sea in ships, and occupy by the great waters, they see the works

of the Lord, and his woonders in the deepe, &c. Which
words of the Prophet together with my cousins discourse (things of high and rare delight to my yong
nature) tooke in me so deepe an impression, that I
constantly resolued, if euer I were preferred to the
Vniuersity, where better time, and more conuenient
place might be ministred for these studies, I would
by Gods assistance prosecute that knowledge and
kinde of literature, the doores whereof (after a sort)
were so happily opened before me."

When he returned to Westminster he was already
famous.   I find him living in a house, now destroyed,
which adjoined the School, where he continued to
pursue his geographical studies.   He became Arch-
deacon of Westminster in 1602, and in 1604 one
of the Chaplains of the Savoy.   He died in 1616
and lies buried in the Abbey Church in a nameless
grave.

In the meantime one of the greatest of English anti-
quarians and historians, William Camden, who had
taught at Westminster first as an usher and then as
head master, from 1575 to 1599, had been working
on somewhat parallel lines to Hakluyt.   Just as it
had been Hakluyt's object " to emphasize the greatness of the English adventurers and of English
initiative," so it was Camden's object to awaken the
interest of his countrymen in the history and beauty
of the English countryside.   In his ' Britannia,' at
which he was working on successive editions amid
the distractions of school life, " he leads his fellow-
countrymen," as it has been said, " along its high roads
and through its towns and cities, faithfully guiding
them amid the hills and dales and rivers and the

monuments of byegone ages, and thus meriting the name of 'the Pausanias of the British Isles.'"*

He tells us himself in a letter to Abp. Usher that he "never set sail after present preferments or desired to soar higher by others," but in 1597 he was appointed Clarenceux King-at-Arms. The appointment was not entirely pleasing to that exclusive body the College of Arms—"he being but a schoolmaster" as one of his future colleagues indignantly wrote. It may perhaps be hinted that there were pedigrees compiled and recorded by the Tudor Heralds which would hardly stand the scrutiny of so careful an antiquary and scholar as William Camden. It was to him as Clarenceux (and to Garter) that John Shakespeare submitted the evidence which resulted in the granting of a coat of arms to him and his successors.

He continued to reside in the precincts after his appointment as Clarenceux "in the new brick buildings on the west part of the College Bakehouse" in the middle of what is now Dean's Yard. In 1600 he published the first official guide-book to the Abbey Church containing a brief account in Latin of the foundation and subsequent history of the Abbey, with short notices of the most notable persons buried within its walls and the epitaphs upon their tombs. Two copies of this work, specially printed on large paper, on the wide margins of which have been tricked by hand the coats of arms of those buried in the Abbey Church, are in existence. One of them, presented by the author to Queen Elizabeth in 1601, is

* 'Shakespeare's England.' Article on Scholarship by Sir John Sandys, vol. i, p. 255.

preserved in the Old Royal Library at the British Museum; the other (which there is some ground for believing to have been his own copy) was purchased with the help of the Friends of the National Libraries and now rests in the Library of Westminster Abbey, of which Camden had himself been the Keeper from 1587 to 1597.*

The most famous of those who received their education at Westminster under Camden was Ben Jonson. For Camden Jonson retained a deep affection. In the first quarto of 'Cynthia's Revels' entitled 'The Fountaine of Selfe-Love' (1601), which Jonson presented to Camden, he describes himself as "Alumnus olim, aeternum Amicus." He dedicated 'Every Man in his Humour' to him, and in a well-known epigram he refers to him as—

> " Camden most reverend head to whom I owe
> All that I am in arts and all I know."†

Ben Jonson's connection with Westminster both at the beginning and end of his life is an interesting one. He was a posthumous child and was probably born in 1572.‡ His most recent biographers have not been able to throw much fresh light on his early life, and seem to accept Fuller's statement that " when a little child he lived in Hartes Horn Lane near Charing Cross where his mother married a bricklayer for her second husband." Malone hazarded a conjecture that an entry of a marriage which he found in the Registers of St. Martin's-in-the-Fields under the date

---

* Cf. ' Annual Report, Friends of National Libraries,' 1936–7, pp. 26–7.
† Cf. ' Shakespeare's England,' vol. ii, p. 210 and note.
‡ Herford and Simpson, ' Ben Jonson,' vol. i, p. 2.

November 17th, 1575 ("Mr Thos Fowler to M^{ris} Margareta Johnson ") referred to this marriage.

Some years ago I ventured to point out* that if Malone's guess is right—and it is supported by the date and by the fact that Mrs. Jonson is described as " Mistress," a designation to which she was entitled as the widow of a gentleman by birth—it was possible to identify " Mr Thos Fowler " and thereby to dispose of the often repeated " bricklayer " story. From our Muniments it seems quite clear that so far from being a bricklayer he was a man of substance and was the " Thomas Fowler of the parish of St. Martin's-in-the-Fields beside Charing Cross, of the County of Middlesex, Gent., and Controller of the Queen's Majesty's Works," who was appointed Surveyor to the Dean and Chapter of Westminster in 1572.† As such he was entirely responsible for the fabric of Westminster Abbey. In 1575 he was living in a house " near the high street " at Charing Cross and he continued to reside within the parish until his death. As the Abbey Surveyor he must have been known to Camden, and it would be natural for the young Jonson to be sent to the school in the Precincts.

There is a tradition that Jonson was taken away from Westminster and apprenticed as a bricklayer to his stepfather ; but this assumes perhaps a somewhat different aspect if the identification of the stepfather with one of the leading architects and surveyors of the time is correct. As we should say to-day, he was merely being given the opportunity of a good opening in his stepfather's profession.

* ' Times Litt. Supp.,' April 1st, 1926.
† W. A. M. 9905.

There is, too, this further point to consider. It is possible that Jonson's home life was not happy, and that this was what he meant—if Drummond reports him correctly—when he told him " he was poorly brought up." In his will* Thomas Fowler speaks of his three wives " Ellen, Margaret and Elizabeth." He cannot have been a man of deep affections. A reference to the registers of St. Martin's shows that " M^{ris} Ellen Fowler " was buried on August 25th, 1575. On November 17th of the same year he married Mrs. Margareta Jonson. " M^{ris} Margareta Fowler," in her turn, was buried on April 2nd, 1590, and within a month, on April 29th, he married his third wife, " Elyzab Powell." It may well be that Jonson, after 1590, with both a stepfather and a stepmother, found life difficult, and that it was this rather than " bricklaying " which " he could not endure " and caused him to go off soldiering in Flanders.

Thomas Fowler died in 1595, and among the Muniments is an inventory of his goods.† He makes no mention of Jonson in his will; but by that time Jonson had married and had chosen his own life.

For my temerity in advancing these theories I was, perhaps rightly, castigated by Dr. Greg, who pointed out the incontrovertible facts that we neither knew the christian name of Jonson's mother nor the surname of his stepfather, and further that if Drummond of Hawthornden is to be trusted Jonson's mother was still living at a date when for the purposes of this theory

---

* W. A. M. 17214, copy of original.
† W. A. M. 17215.

it would have been more convenient if she had been in her grave.*

But like Cowper's resilient friend, " I am confuted but not entirely convinced " ! At the least I venture to think that the theory is an interesting one. Drummond is not infallible as to dates,† and it does, or it may, throw some light on this period of Jonson's career.

But however this may be—and perhaps we may leave it with the verdict " not proven "—we do know that in his old age Jonson came back to Westminster and lived, as Aubrey tells us, "in the house under wch you passe, as you goe out of the Church yard into the old Palace."‡ As it happens, our records at the Abbey enable us to identify the site of this house, long since destroyed, with some precision. It stood between St. Margaret's Church and Henry VII's Chapel, and was formerly known as the Talbot. It consisted of four rooms on the ground, first and second floors with garrets over them. There was also a yard where, as we know from one of his letters, Jonson kept a tame fox.§ One of the rooms on the first floor is particularly described in a deed of sale of 1650 as being " over the passage leading from the old Palace into the Churchyard."|| The house belonged to the Dean and Chapter, and at the time

---

* ' Times Litt. Supp.,' April 8th, 1926. See also ' L.C.C. Survey of London,' vol. xviii, p. 22 n., which considers that my conjecture " may represent the truth." The objection mentioned there in connection with Thomas Fowler's house can be disposed of by the fact that he did not take this particular house until 1592 ('West. Abbey Reg.,' Book XV, pp. 68–69.)

† It must be remembered, too, that the original MS. of Drummond's talks does not exist.

‡ Quoted in Herford and Simpson's ' Ben Jonson,' vol. i, p. 179.

§ *Ibid.*, vol. i, p. 213.

|| W. A. M. 36331. See also a plan of the whole house in 1723.

that Jonson lived there the tenant was Sir Richard
Manley, whose son and granddaughter find a place
in the 'Dictionary of National Biography'. It
appears however to have been sublet to a nameless
old lady with whom Jonson boarded. She, if the
gossip of Aubrey and others is to be believed, collected
Jonson's pension and shared in his potations.

In this house, surrounded by his books, he lived
the last twelve years of his life, most of the time in
dire poverty—and in this connection it is pleasant
to remember that in his hour of greatest need, when
he was first struck down by paralysis, the Dean and
Chapter sent him £5 to relieve his immediate necessities.* But throughout the time he was never
lacking in friends and he had the run of Sir Robert
Cotton's library and manuscripts, which were housed
in the old Palace of Westminster and within a few
minutes of his door.† We have some glimpses of him
at this time in James Howell's 'Familiar Epistles.'
Howell seems to have lived next door to him for a
time. In one of his letters to him he signs himself
" your son and contiguous neighbour," and desires
him " to look better hereafter to your charcoal fire
and chimney which I am glad to be one that preserved
it from burning."‡ He also sketches this vivid little
picture of him in a letter to Sir Thomas Hawke :

" I was invited yesternight to a solemn supper by
Ben Jonson . . . there was good company, excellent chear, choice wines and jovial welcome. One

---

* W. A. M. 34163, f. 44 : " Given . . . to Mr Benjamin Jhonson
in his sicknes and want . . . 5li " (Accompt Book of Treasurer);
cf. Herford and Simpson, vol. i, p. 244.
† " Coming into Sir Robert Cotton's house as he often doth," quoted
Herford and Simpson, vol. i, p. 242.
‡ Letter dated June 27th, 1629.

thing interven'd, which almost spoil'd the relish of
the rest that B. began to engross all the discourse, to
vapour extremely of himself, and by vilifying others,
to magnify his own Muse."*

There is something rather pathetic in the picture of
the old poet, the acknowledged leader of the literary
world, " vapouring extremely " to his young and
perhaps unappreciative friends of the mighty contemporaries whom he had outlived.

A year later, on August 6th, 1637, he, too, was to
seek " the undiscovered country " and to be laid to
rest in the Abbey Church.   According to a local
tradition he had begged the King, Charles I, to grant
him a favour.   "What is it ?" said the King.   "Give
me eighteen inches of square ground."   " Where ? "
asked the King.   " In Westminster Abbey."   In
consequence of this he was supposed to have been
buried upright.

In 1849, when the grave of Sir Robert Wilson was
being dug nearby, the Dean, Dr. Buckland, was
anxious to test the truth of the tradition, and gave
orders that particular care was to be taken.   In due
course the workmen found a coffin much decayed
which appeared to have been buried in an upright
position, and as they proceeded the loose sand
" rippled in like quicksand " revealing two leg bones
fixed bolt upright, while a skull came " rolling down
among the sand " from a position above them.   The
Clerk of the Works took charge of this skull, which
had still some red hair on it, and subsequently
replaced it in the grave.   It was seen again at the
burial of John Hunter in 1859, and was again re-buried

* Letter dated April 5th, 1636.

" some twelve or eighteen inches " under the tri-
angular stone which marks Ben Jonson's grave, and
there presumably it rests to-day.*

There is one further point before we leave Ben
Jonson. From time to time a correspondence is
started in the newspapers whether the famous inscription on the stone is really " O Rare Ben Jonson," or
as the writers would like to believe—in defiance of
latinity—" Orare Ben Jonson." It is perhaps worth
while to try and settle the matter. In the first place
it may be noted that until recent years no one has
ever disputed the ordinary interpretation. The
accepted story, for which Aubrey is the authority, is
that Jonson was buried in the nave of the Abbey
" with this inscription only on him, in a pavement
square of blew marble, about fourteen inches square :

O rare Benn Johnson

wch was donne at the chardge of Jack Young, afterwards Knighted, who walking there when the grave
was covering gave the fellow eighteen pence to cutt
it."†

There is a curious and interesting tradition that
the rather unusual phrase arose from the popular
applause which greeted his play ' Bartholomew Fair,'
in contrast to the somewhat cold reception by the
audience of his previous play, ' Catiline,'‡ but be
this as it may, it is a fact that when Sir William
Davenant, Jonson's friend and successor as Laureate,

---

* For the whole story of Frank Buckland's account of how he took
charge of another skull which was found at the time under the impression
that it was Jonson's see Buckland's ' Curiosities of Natural History '
(4th series), ed. 1905, pp. 238–248.

† J. Aubrey, ' Brief Lives . . . ', ed. 1898, vol. ii, p. 13.

‡ Herford and Simpson, p. 183 n. 46.

came to be buried in the Abbey in 1668, the inscription cut on his gravestone was (and is) " O rare Sir William Davenant," in imitation of the inscription on Ben Jonson.

The original stone which covered Ben Jonson was removed when the Nave was repaved, but was found a few years later by Dean Buckland, and is now let into the wall beneath the riser of the stone seat a few feet away from the grave. It is quite obvious from the fact that there is a space of $1\frac{3}{4}$ to 2 inches between the " O " and the " rare " that they were meant to be two words, and these facts would seem to be conclusive that the traditional interpretation is the right one.

*   *   *

We must retrace our steps. As we have mentioned, Ben Jonson lived over the gate leading from the Sanctuary to the Old Palace. At the other or western end of the Sanctuary there stood, until 1776, a somewhat grim-looking Gatehouse. It consisted of two vaulted entries standing at right angles to each other, one leading from Tothill Street to the Sanctuary and the other from the Sanctuary to the precincts of the Monastery. It had been built in the fourteenth century and the upper part was used as a prison, as indeed had been the previous Gatehouse which stood on the site. Among the Abbey Muniments is an inventory of the contents of the Prison in 1379, and among the prison gear are such sinister objects as a " bolt of thick iron called Saint Petrysbotes with 3 iron shackles belonging thereto."*   It was under the control first of the Abbots and later of the Deans of

* W. A. M. 17699.

Westminster, and something had been done by the beginning of the seventeenth century to improve the accommodation. There was a portion set aside for more important prisoners, and thither was brought Sir Walter Raleigh on the evening of October 28th, 1618, to spend his last night on earth. We derive almost all our knowledge of his last hours and execution from the Dean of Westminster, Dr. Tounson, who was ordered to attend him both in the prison and on the scaffold, and it was to the Dean that Raleigh left instructions that the lovely lines which he wrote in those last sad hours should be delivered :

> " Even such is Time, that takes in trust
> Our youth, our joys, our all we have,
> And pays us but with earth and dust ;
> Who in the dark and silent grave,
> When we have wander'd all our ways,
> Shuts up the story of our days ;
> But from this earth, this grave, this dust,
> My God shall raise me up, I trust."

In a long letter to Sir Justinian Isham* the Dean expresses his astonishment at Raleigh's courage: " When I begann to encourage him against the feare of death, he seemed to make so light of itt that I wondered at him," and he adds, " He was the most fearless of death that ever was known." Even on the morning of his execution " he was very cheerfull . . . tooke tobacco . . . and made no more of his death, than it had bene to take a journey ; and left a great impression in the minds of those that beheld him." The Dean accompanied him to

* E. Edwards, ' Life of Sir Walter Raleigh,' vol. ii, p. 489 ; *cf.* vol. i, p. 693.

the scaffold, which was set up in Old Palace Yard.*
His body lies buried in St. Margaret's Church.

Once more the grim Gatehouse was to inspire
immortal verse. In 1642 Richard Lovelace was
committed to the Gatehouse for presenting to
Parliament a petition on behalf of the King. And
there he wrote ('To Althea from Prison') the famous
lines—

> "Stone walls do not a prison make,
> Nor iron bars a cage ;
> Minds innocent and quiet take
> That for a hermitage ;
> If I have freedom in my love
> And in my soul am free,
> Angels alone, that soar above,
> Enjoy such liberty."

His imprisonment was short, and after about seven
weeks in the Gatehouse he was released on petitioning
that he might be allowed to serve against the rebels
in Ireland.

The Civil Wars made all but a clean sweep of those
who held authority within the precincts of the Abbey.
One man, and one man alone, survived from earlier
days. At the Restoration Dr. Busby had been Head
Master of Westminster for 22 years ; he was to continue to rule the school with unchallenged authority
for a further period of 35 years. During that long
period no one had ever doubted either his loyalty to
the King, even during the Commonwealth, or his
intense devotion to the cause of education. You will

* Edwards, *op. cit.*, p. 699 : " Having proceeded thus far [in his speech]
he explained to the Lords in Sir Randolph Carew's [Crewe's] balcorney his
fear about the audibleness of his voice." This shows that the scaffold
must have been erected about opposite to the Peers' Entrance and rather
towards the W. and Abingdon St., for it is possible from the Abbey
Muniments to identify the site of Sir Randolph Crewe's house.

remember that it was before his monument in the Abbey that Addison made Sir Roger de Coverley pause and exclaim, "Dr. Busby, a great man"—and then as the full measure of that greatness dawned on him he added, "He whipped my grandfather ; a *very* Great Man ! "   At the Restoration he had been made a Prebendary and Treasurer of the Abbey, and in this last capacity it fell to him to deal with the Abbey properties to evolve order from the confusion of Civil War and Commonwealth, and to endeavour to set the Abbey finances again on a sound basis.   It is not surprising, therefore, to find William Ashburnham, who had settled in the house in the Precincts which still bears his name, gossiping with his friend Pepys and telling him " odd stories how he was dealt with by the men of the Church at Westminster in taking a lease of them . . .   and particularly the devilish covetousness of Dr. Busby "*—appreciation of financial efficiency had never been numbered among the cavalier virtues.

Pepys himself, at the time of the Restoration and until September, 1660, was living in Axe Yard, a turning out of King Street, Westminster, and must have been a familiar figure about the Precincts.   He tells us much that is of interest concerning the Abbey in the early days of the reign of Charles II.   He meets with one of the Abbey clergy and is taken in among the choir and " there sang with them their service "† ; he goes to hear Mr. Rowe preach, and " in the midst of the sermon some plaster fell from the top of the Abbey, that made me and all the rest in

* ' Diary,' May 3rd, 1667.
† *Ibid.*, December 29th, 1661.

our pew afeard, and I wished myself out "*; he hears
the organs, " the first time that ever I heard organs
in a Cathedral "†; and he gives us a vivid account
of the Coronation of Charles II, which he saw from a
gallery in the N. Transept.‡ He was also a constant
attendant at the parish church of St. Margaret's and
a caustic critic of the sermons he heard there : " 1666.
May 13 (Lord's Day) . . .   St. Margaret's Church
where I heard a young man play the foole upon the
doctrine of purgatory."

Nor, it must be confessed, was it only the sermons
which attracted him : " 1667.   May 26 (Lord's Day)
. . .   After dinner I by water alone to Westminster,
where, not finding Mrs Martin within, did go towards
the parish church, and in the way did overtake her,
who resolved to go into the church with her that she
was going with . . .   and then go out again, and
so I to the church, and seeing her return did go out
again myself, but met with Mr. Howlett, who, offering
me a pew in the gallery, I had no excuse but up with
him I must go, and then much against my will staid
out the whole church in pain while she expected me
at home, but I did entertain myself with my perspective glass up and down the church, by which I
had the great pleasure of seeing and gazing at a great
many very fine women ; and what with that, and
sleeping, I passed away the time till sermon was done,
and then to Mrs. Martin . . ."

Pepys's eager curiosity was better employed when
meeting one day with his friend, Dr. Christopher
Gibbons, the Abbey Organist, they went together to

* *Ibid.*, September 23rd, 1660.
† *Ibid.*, November 4th, 1660.
‡ *Ibid.*, April 23rd, 1661.

call on Dr. Dolben, the Dean of Westminster, in order to see an organ of which the Dean was anxious to dispose.   The organ proved to be too big for Pepys's house, but he noted that the Dean " lived like a great prelate, his lodgings being very good," and he was amused by the Dean's two children, " whereof one [was] a very pretty little boy, like him, so fat and black."*   Dolben, who while still an undergraduate had fought for the King and been wounded at Marston Moor, was to become Archbishop of York.   He is commemorated in Dryden's ' Absolom and Ahitophel ' as—

> " Him of the Western Dome, whose weighty sense
> Flows in fit words and heavenly eloquence."

His fame as a preacher was, however, equalled, if not excelled, by the Sub-Dean, Robert South.   It was before South that an aspiring but disappointed curate (could it have been Pepys's young man ?) is said to have preached from the text " Promotion cometh neither from the East nor the West nor from *the* South."   South outlived all his contemporaries, and his long expected death, when at length it occurred, provoked an incident which caused an immense stir in the literary world of the time.   The notorious publisher, Edmund Curll, obtained an inaccurate copy of the Latin Funeral Oration which the Captain of Westminster had pronounced in honour of South, and published it without permission and without correction.   A few days later he was incautious enough to venture within the precincts of the school. He was caught by the King's Scholars, made to sue for pardon on his knees, tossed in a blanket, flogged

* *Ibid.*, February 24th, 1667/8.

and kicked out of the Yard.   The punishment meted out to him delighted Pope and others who had suffered from Curll's piratical tendencies.   It was made the subject of a satiric poem, "'Neck or Nothing,' a consolatory letter . . . to Mr. C—ll " from the pen of Samuel Wesley, who was then an usher at the School.   Wesley had much of the vigour and poetic gifts of his more famous brothers, but was suspected of Jacobitism.   He therefore failed to scale the ladder of promotion, and after twenty years at Westminster subsided into the Head Mastership of Blundell's School at Tiverton.   His poetic mantle descended to his colleague at Westminster, Vincent Bourne, a Latin poet of great charm, " a sweet unpretending pretty-mannered *matterful* creature " as Charles Lamb called him in a letter to Wordsworth, " sucking from every flower, making a flower of everything, his diction all Latin and his thoughts all English."*

" I love the memory of Vinny Bourne," wrote Cowper, " I think him a better Latin Poet than Tibullus and Propertius, Ausonias or any of the writers in his way except Ovid and not at all inferior to *him*.   I love him too with a love of partiality, because he was Usher of the Fifth Form at West-minster when I passed through it.   He was so good-natured and so indolent, that I lost more than I got by him ; for he made me as idle as himself " ; and he adds, " I remember seeing the Duke of Richmond set fire to his greasy locks and box his ears to put it out again."

It is pleasant to remember the many happy refer-ences to his schooldays in Cowper's letters, and it is

* ' Lamb's Letters,' ed. E. V. Lucas, vol. vi, p. 457.

now generally admitted that ' Tirocinium ' was aimed
not at Westminster, but at a system of which he had
come to disapprove in later life.   It comes almost as
a shock to find that instead of a timid gentle shrinking
" stricken deer," Cowper was in fact in his last year
at Westminster third in the VIth Form and head of
his House.   It can be gathered from references in
his letters that at this period of his life he rode, shot,
swam, danced all night, and still more surprising—
but they are his own words—that " he excelled at
cricket and football."   We are apt to forget, as the
late Mr. John Sargeaunt remarked, " the dilapidating
effects of love, lunacy and John Newton."*   The
most conspicuous event of his schooldays must have
been the building and completion of the western
towers of the Abbey, and it may well have been
while watching their progress that his eye fell on a
tombstone which almost within living memory still
stood prominently in St. Margaret's Churchyard and
bore the immortal name " Mr John Gilpin."

The Dean (Wilcocks) was so delighted with his
towers that he refused further promotion in order
to watch over the completion of the Western Front,
and they are represented both in his picture at the
Deanery and on his monument at the Abbey.   His
enthusiasm has not perhaps been shared by later
ages.

His successor, Zachary Pearce, was a man of rather
different type.   A profound scholar, he is remembered
as " the only person who gave Johnson any assistance
in the Compilation of his Dictionary."†   In later

* Sargeaunt, ' Annals of Westminster School,' p. 133.
† ' Boswell ' (ed. B. Hill), vol. i, p. 292 ; vol. iii, p. 112.

years they probably met at the house in the Precincts which belonged to Johnson's lifelong friend, Dr. John Taylor, who was a Prebendary of Westminster from 1746 to 1788.

At first Taylor lived in the house, later known as Turles, of which only the front door in the Dark Cloister now remains.   Later, in 1760, he moved to a charming house (No. 20) in Dean's Yard, which remains very much as it was in his day.   At both houses Johnson was a frequent visitor.

The friendship was a strange one.   In all outward respects Taylor was everything that Johnson most disliked.   He was a Whig, a worldly self-seeking pluralist, living in comfort and luxury, fond of the pleasures of the table, interested mainly in his farm at his country living at Ashbourne in Derbyshire, without any conversational powers " his talk " as Johnson said " is mainly of bullocks "—and with a disconcerting habit of going off to bed at an early hour, " very disagreeable to a man who likes to fold his legs and have his talk out, as I do."

And yet in spite of his shortcomings, or perhaps because of them, Johnson never ceased to regard him with affection, and to insist that he was " a very sensible acute man and had a strong mind."   For many years he scarcely ever failed to pay him an annual visit at Ashbourne, and to be greatly amused by the fact—as he put it—that " his whole system is so different from mine that we seemed formed for different elements."   He allowed himself to be shown the farm, and praised and criticized the live-stock. " I have seen the great bull," he writes to Mrs. Thrale, " and very great he is.   I have seen likewise his heir apparent, who promises to inherit all the bulk and all the virtues of his sire "—and he had no sort of use for the tactless neighbour who insisted that he had seen a bigger bull than Taylor's.

The pages in which Boswell describes the visit that he and Johnson paid to Ashbourne in 1777 are some of the most delightful in the ' Life,' and even Boswell was forced to admit that he had seldom if ever seen Johnson " more uniformly social, cheerful and alert." He records a discussion on politics when, much to his amusement, host and guest " were roused . . . to a pitch of bellowing " which would have been terrifying if it had not been so good humoured. For no quarrel ever disturbed their friendship. He was, in truth, the one man with whom Johnson could talk of the past, for they had been at school and Oxford together, and, as he remarked, Taylor was better acquainted with his heart than any man or woman alive.

He, perhaps alone of Johnson's friends, had realized how deeply Johnson loved his wife, and when the news of her death was brought to him at his house in the Cloisters at 3 o'clock in the morning, he had risen at once and gone to his friend in his distress. Such acts of friendship are not easily forgotten.

"Forsitan et nostrum nomen miscebitur istis."

Goldsmith rests elsewhere, but his sculptured bust above the epitaph which Johnson wrote on him (with the famous line, " Nullum quod tetigit non ornavit ") looks down on the spot where many years before he and Johnson had stood together and where Johnson himself was laid to rest in 1784. And on that

December day it was Taylor who read the burial service over his lifelong friend. One cannot doubt that it was what Johnson would himself have wished.

The death of Johnson may be said to have closed a literary epoch, and it is perhaps a suitable place to bring these rather discursive notes to a close. I have limited myself to some of those who were prominent in the sixteenth, seventeenth and eighteenth centuries, but it is well to remember that these literary links can be traced back to a remote past, that Chaucer and Caxton lived within the precincts of the Monastery, that Spenser died within a stone's throw of the Abbey Church, and that the connection between the Abbey and those famous in the annals of literature has continued unbroken to the present day.

" FUGITIVE POETRY."

An Eighteenth Century Collection.

BY N. HARDY WALLIS, M.A., F.R.S.L.

[Read December 14th, 1938.]

THE little volumes which I wish to bring to your
attention this afternoon belong to the numerous
collections of verse which were published during the
last decades of the eighteenth century, when the
springs of poetry were running low, and were hardly
yet fed by the flow and fullness of the so-called
" Romantic Revival." These anthologies were
extensive if not exclusive, and political or social
distinction was often made a justification for the
inclusion of a poem, when the actual effusion was
either a worthless imitation of Pope, or an " Ode " with
the manner but not the mastery of Dryden.

This is indeed true of the present collection, for the
Editor was evidently determined to include as many
nearly contemporary versifiers as possible, quite
regardless of the merit or the subject of their poems ; in
fact Mr John Bell, to whose industry these volumes
are due, was a gentleman of more enthusiasm than

taste, of more patriotism than judgment, as his prefatory quotation will reveal :

> Though redolent of ev'ry flower
> That once perfum'd Hymettus' side,
> No hoarded sweets of Greecian store
> Did ere the Attic bee provide,
> That could a purer flavor yield,
> Than yields the comb this hive contains,
> Though cull'd from no Hesperian field,
> But the wild growth of Britain's plains.

Our compiler was born in 1745 and died in 1831. He seems to have had a passion for publishing collections, and was responsible for the one hundred and nine volumes of 'Bell's British Poets' (1777–1782) and for a gathering of Plays entitled 'The British Theatre.' He was also the founder of Bell's *Weekly Messenger*, a popular periodical and a pioneer in the production of cheap books ; while being a man of modern outlook he initiated the abolition of the long " s " in typography.

The collection of verse entitled 'Fugitive Poetry' came into my hands after the death of a friend, and forms a series of six dumpy and fat little volumes, in which the separate books are bound together in groups of three. The bindings are of brown calf and they are labelled in black and red, as were the cherished possession of Chaucer's 'Clerk.'

The eighteenth century fondness for classification shows clearly in the grouping of the poems under headings. We have 'Epistles,' 'Elegies' and 'Odes' each with their sub-headings, of which the more quaint may be mentioned. The first class are

' Epistles Familiar and Humorous,' ' Epistles Panegyrical and Gallant,' ' Epistles Heroic and Amatory ' ; the second have the title ' Elegies, Moral, Descriptive and Amatory,' ' Elegies Local and Sympathetic ' ; while the Odes are separated into classes numbered 1 to 10, a division which it would appear has nothing to do with their merit or subject. The whole collection contains some five hundred poems.

Here then is plentiful harvest of late eighteenth century poetry for the gleaner, but few of the ears yield much grain. However, let me attempt to gather a sheaf of characteristic effusions, not only because they are interesting in themselves, but also because they will show to what levels of bathos the writers could descend. Many of the verses are amusing in the efforts made by their authors to show the reader that they have closely studied the balance of the decasyllabic couplet, and most of the ' Epistles ' are composed in this metre, which lends itself to their favourite themes—flattery and eulogy. In the ' Odes ' and ' Elegies ' a greater freedom of rhythm is permitted and the irregular lines of Dryden in such an ' Ode ' as that on ' Alexander's Feast,' are used for the purpose of platitude, if not of poetry.

The collection is not without some well-known names, such as those of Johnson, Parnell, Beattie and the Wartons, but these poets, although something of an aristocracy, have contributed little that is better than the effusions of the minor writers whose names are little known even to the student of the period.

For example there is Mr. Alsop. This poet took his M.A. at Christchurch in 1696, and his B.D. in 1706. He published his selections from ' Aesop ' in 1698,

and became a Prebendary of Winchester and Rector
of Brightwell in Berkshire. The chief event of his life
may be shortly summarized : " He left England on
losing an action for breach of promise of marriage,
returned and met his death by drowning." John Bell,
however, in his ' Notes,' gives more light on this
tragic end. " At Brightwell, Mr. Alsop, notwith-
standing the solicitations of his friends, sequestered
himself for the rest of his life, which was terminated in
1726 by a fall into a ditch from a narrow path leading
to his garden door."

Mr. Alsop's ' Epistle ' is addressed to the Rev. Sir
John Dolben, and deals with a projected visit to his
friend's seat at Finedon ; which is impossible owing
to the inertia of the poet :

> But miles there are twenty and thirty,
> Both woundy long, and plaguy dirty,
> Which I, the laziest thing alive,
> Could scarcely pass in days twice five.

He comforts himself with the thought of the feast that
he would receive on arrival :

> Then woe be to the beef and claret
> For by my faith I would not spare it ;
> Nor should I, once possession taken,
> Contrive or care to save your bacon,

—but suddenly realizes that he is a " sot " to think of
food or drink when he might by his journey see the
beauty of his host's family :

> How should I joy to see the Lady
> That makes three sweet ones call you Dady !
> To see those pretty heirs apparent
> Trip it along like fairies errant !

After this " delightful simile " he wanders on until we
agree with his last lines :

> Thus having tir'd myself and you, Sir,
> I kiss your hands, and so adieu, Sir !

Then there is James Bramston (1694–1744), of whom
little is known. He contributes to our anthology
two long poems, ' The Man of Taste ' and the ' Art of
Politics,' which are written in easy couplets, and of
which the latter has some satirical touches not so
out-of-date as might be expected :

> It must be own'd the journals try all ways
> To merit their respective party's praise :
> They jar in every article from Spain ;
> A war these threaten, those a peace maintain ;
> Though be they will, to give them all their due,
> In foreign matters and domestic, too.
> But truth is scarce, the scene of action large,
> And correspondence an excessive charge !

and :

> A politician must (as I have read)
> Be furnished in the first place with a head
> A head well fill'd with Machiavelian brains
> And stuff'd with precedents of former reigns.
> Give to his country what's his country's due—
> But first help brothers, sons, and cousins too !

Even the medical faculty does not escape his wit :

> In all professions, time and pains give skill—
> Without hard study dare physicians kill ?

Bramston is also the author of an amusing ' Epistle to Captain Hinton,' giving him dietetic advice ;

> Hinton, old friend, accept from me
> The following rules without a fee ;
> An asthma is your case I think,
> So you must neither eat nor drink ;
> I mean of meats preserv'd in salt,
> Nor any liquor made of malt ;
> From season'd sauce avert your eyes,
> From hams, and tongues, and pigeon-pies ;
> If venison-pasty's set before ye
> Each bit you eat—memento mori.

And stating sound sense when he adds :

> Let constant exercise be tried,
> And sometimes walk and sometimes ride,
> Health oftener comes from Blackdown Hill
> Than from th' apothecary's bill.

Such rules should appeal to the present day and to those who wish to " make hay while the fool dines." It has been mentioned that James Beattie (1735–1803) is one of the contributors to ' Fugitive Poetry,' and the collection includes his ' Minstrel ' (1771) and other productions, but omits to print his ' Hermit,' which is remarkable for having reduced Dr. Johnson to tears. " Such was his sensibility, and so much was he affected by pathetic poetry that, when he was reading Dr. Beattie's ' Hermit ' in my presence, it brought tears into his eyes " (Boswell, 1783). It is difficult to imagine ' The Minstrel ' causing such distress, for this production, in two books and ninety-three stanzas in imitation of Spenser, is a mingling of lines which sometimes rise to real poetry, but are more often conventional in the extreme. This is not the moment for a careful analysis of the poem, but a few stanzas may be mentioned to show that the writer " could not keep heights his soul was competent to gain." The poet who could create the musical lines,

> Far to the west the long long vale withdrawn,
> Where twilight loves to linger for a while,

or the Shelleyan phrase,

> For now the storm howls mournful through the brake,
> And the dead foliage flies in many a shapeless flake

was also guilty of these :

> Where the grey linnets carol from the hill
> O let them ne'er with artificial note
> To please a tyrant, strain the little bill,

and even of worse :

> Fancy now no more
> Wantons on fickle pinion through the skies,
> But fix'd in aim, and conscious of her power
> Sublime from cause to cause exults to rise,
> Creation's blended stores arranging as she flies.

The picture called up by these lines is delightfully vague, but it is comforting to know that " Fancy " has an orderly mind even in a commercial plane.

Other sudden descents from the sublime to the ridiculous may be found in the effusions of Beattie. In an ' Elegy ' on the popular subject of ' Melancholy,' the poet, after an address to ' Liberty ' ending with the line—

> O'er her expiring son the Goddess mourns,

returns to his subject :

> Still Grief recoils. How vainly have I strove
> Thy power, O Melancholy, to withstand !
> Tir'd I submit, but yet, O yet remove
> Or ease the pressure of thy heavy hand !

Imitations of Spenser were frequent at this time, and another may be noticed by a certain Robert Bedingfield, of whom, as of so many other writers in this anthology, little can be discovered. His contribution is a long poem on ' The Education of Achilles.' The infant hero is brought by Thetis to a " grott " where various personified Virtues instruct him. As might be expected, we find Modesty, Temperance, Fidelity and Benevolence in attendance, and lest this should seem too feminine a group, the masculine protagonists of Exercise, Experience and Contemplation. Each is described in turn. Exercise :

> Reclin'd he seem'd upon his rough boar-spear
> As late surceas'd from hardy enterprise.

Modesty, or should it be Censorship ?

> Fast by the cave a damsel was ypight,
> Afraid from earth her blushing looks to rear,
> Lest aught indecent should offend her sight,
> Lest aught indecent should offend her ear.

Contemplation seems to have been a vigorous old gentleman :

> Yet age's hand mote not empare the sight,
> Still with sharp ken the eagle he'd pursue
> As through the buxom air to heav'n's bright bowers
> she flew.

Under these masculine Mentors, for the ladies seem to have given up a hopeless task, and with Exercise as his Physical Instructor, we learn that Achilles (who is never mentioned by name in the poem) became an athletic youth with a great taste for slaughter, which, to judge from Homer, landed him later in much trouble.

Several of the writers in 'Fugitive Poetry' choose Politics for their subject, and one of the most amazing excursions into this field is that of Sir William Browne (1692–1774). This gentleman took his M.D. in 1721, practised at Lynn, and, removing to London, was knighted on becoming President of the College of Physicians. He was the founder of the "Browne Medals," one of which was later won by Frederick Tennyson with a Greek Ode on Egypt. Browne was the author of "sundry verses and orations," and his contribution to this collection is an 'Ode to Sir Robert Walpole on his Ceasing to be Minister.' Bell places it among 'Odes of the Seventh Class,' but surely it should stand alone as a perfect example of artificial versifying ? It opens thus :

> The Minister that's brave and just,
> True to his King's and Country's trust,
>   Defies the tyrant Faction :
> Howe'er its many heads may stare,
> Grown dreadful with a Gorgon air
>   Of general distraction.

The poet laments that the country knows nothing of its greatest men :

> Thus Somers, for past service done,
> Thus Marlborough, for realms o'errun,
>   Were by their Country treated,
> Who now quaff Nectar's flowing tide,
> With just Godolphin by their side,
>   Celestially seated.

Here is a lovely picture of " heavenly harmony."
But it is soon disturbed, and by no less a person than
the King :

> George thus addressed his brother Gods,
> Assembled in their blest abodes
>   And Britain's fate debating :
> ' Long have the Stuarts ceas'd to reign,
> Since James' Priests and foreign Queen
>   Drove on his abdicating.
>
> ' The bigot King shall now no more
> Hold commerce with Rome's scarlet Whore
>   And back her superstition.
> No more shall Stuart's perjur'd house
> Britain's credulity abuse
>   While plotting her perdition.'

George seems to have a vindictive memory in his
happy state of immortality !   But worse is to come :

> Nay, frauds forgotten, I'm content
> He should be rank'd in right descent ;
>   Let but the British Ocean
> Still roar between his sons and mine
> And let the royal exiles reign
>   Where they can find promotion.

Britain is going to be very busy :

> Her fleets shall all around proclaim
> To distant shores her dreaded name
>   In peals of British thunder.
> Cross from the Old World to the New,
> There sails shall fly, her fame pursue
>   And fill both worlds with wonder.

But her most Christian and deeply lamented Monarch will have his terms :

> But these great things that I relate
> Can only be her glorious fate
>   On this express condition :
> That with false zeal no more she burns,
> No more to Stuart's race returns
>   And Papal imposition.

The apotheosized King, after this statement, is guilty of the crime of rhyming " Freedom " with " blood'em " ; and the poet gives us a rest from his spiteful remarks in his final verse :

> But whither would my Muse aspire ?
> Forbear to tune the merry lyre
>   To themes past thy attaining ;
> For to attempt in humble odes
> The acts of Heroes, speech of Gods,
>   At best is but profaning.

To which the reader replies with thankfulness, " Amen." Sir William may have been a fine physician —but what a poem.

Gardening and botany were two favourite subjects in the eighteenth century. Was not Darwin's ' Loves of the Plants ' published in 1789, and shall John Bell not include a writer who addresses the Professor of these subjects at Oxford ? Indeed, yes—and his name is Abel Evans, D.D. (1679–1737). His career seems to have been as follows : He was a Probationer of St. John's, Oxford, and, later on taking orders and his D.D. in 1711, was made Chaplain of that college. For some reason he was expelled from this post, but

was later reinstated by the influence of the Duchess
of Marlborough. He was not only known as an
epigrammatist, but also as the author of a satire
called ' The Apparition,' a dialogue betwixt the Devil
and a Doctor concerning the rights of the Christian
Church.

The poem given in ' Fugitive Poetry ' is neither
epigrammatic nor satirical, but entitled ' Vertumnus,'
and addressed to a Mr. Jacob Bobart, the then Curator
of the Physic Garden at Oxford. It opens with some
sane remarks on peace :

> Thank Heaven ! at last our wars are o'er ;
> We're very wise, and very poor :
> All our campaigns at once are done :
> We've ended where we just begun,
> In perfect peace : long may it last
> And pay for all the taxes past !

and then passes on to the subject of the poem. After
dismissing " the pomp and panoply of glorious war,"
the poet writes :

> An honest Muse alike disclaims
> Such authors and their impious themes ;
> And, with a more becoming grace,
> Her song impartial will address,
> Bobart, to thee, the Muses' friend :
> Bobart, the promis'd song attend.

Now for the " promis'd song." After an invocation
to Nature and a description of how :—

> The vallies laugh, the rivers play
> In honour of the God of day,

the poet emphasizes that if it were not for sun and
rain, his friends' labours would be fruitless, but

points out that the Deity could do little without Mr. Bobart !

> Thou, next to him, art truly great,
> On earth his mighty delegate ;
> The vegetable world to guide,
> And o'er all Botany to preside.

He then describes the horticulturist's search for rare seeds, and meanders on in couplets until we arrive at the building of the Portico to the Garden, of which construction he writes :

> The work of Jones' master hand,
> Jones, the Vitruvius of our land.
> He drew the plan, the fabrick fix'd
> With equal strength and beauty mix'd ;
> With perfect symmetry design'd,
> Consummate like the donor's mind.

This is not Wordsworth's Jones who came from Calais (" Jones when we came from Calais, you and I "), but Inigo, the architect admired of eighteenth century authors. Now the poet tells the Botanist that his post is no idle sinecure :

> This makes thee rouse at prime of day
> Thy doubtful nursery to survey,
> At noon to count thy flock with care,
> And in their joys and sorrows share,
> Be ready to attend their cry,
> And all their little wants supply ;
> By day severest sentry keep,
> By night sit by them as they sleep.

The picture of a Professor of Horticulture sitting watchful by a drowsy primula is very delightful !

But the writer realizes that his flattery must include

a mention of the learned works by Mr. Bobart, and, choosing his chief compilation, he praises it in the following words :

> Their barks, or roots, their flowers, or leaves,
> Thy Hortus Siccus still receives !
> In tomes twice ten, that work immense !
> By thee compiled at vast expence ;
> With utmost diligence ammass'd,
> And shall as many ages last.

The poem concludes with this picture :

> And now, methinks, my genius sees
> My friend, amidst his plants and trees ;
> Full in the center there he stands,
> Encircled with his verdant bands ;
> Who all around obsequious wait,
> To know their pleasure and their fate :
> His royal orders to receive,
> To grow, decay, to die, or live :
> That not the proudest kings can boast
> A greater, or more duteous host.

After a visit to a Garden, now for a visit to a Coal-Mine. Dr. John Dalton (1709–1763) was, according to Bell, Tutor to Lord Viscount Beauchamp. He was educated at Queens' College, Oxford, and, after taking his Doctor's degree in the year 1750, became Prebendary of Worcester and rector of St. Mary at Hill, London. Our Editor adds : " Besides his poems in these volumes, he obliged the public with a volume of Sermons, and adapted to the theatre the Comus of Milton."

Let him oblige us with a description of how " Two Ladies returned from viewing the Mines near Whitehaven," the Ladies being the " Honourable Miss

Lowthers, daughters of the late Lord Lonsdale." (The writers in ' Fugitive Poetry ' loved titles !)   It begins :

> Welcome to light, advent'rous pair !
> Thrice welcome to the balmy air
> From sulph'rous damps in caverns deep,
> Where subterranean thunders sleep,
> From bursting streams, and burning rocks,
> From nature's fierce intestine shocks ;
> From the dark mansions of despair,
> Welcome once more to light and air !

And relates how, on the ladies' arrival in the pit, the miners cease work :

> For at your presence toil is o'er,
> The restless miner works no more.
> But quits it now, and hastes away
> To this gay Stygian holiday.
> Agape the sooty collier stands,
> His axe suspended in his hands,
> To see two goddesses so fair
> Descend to him from fields of air.

After this eulogy of the " sisters," the poet proceeds to give an interesting and apparently accurate description of a mine in the eighteenth century :

> Then with increasing wonder gaze,
> The dark inextricable maze,
> Where cavern crossing cavern meets,
> City of subterranean streets.
>
> Your progress next the wondering Muse
> Through narrow galleries pursues ;
> Where Earth the miner's way to close
> Did once the massy rock oppose :
> In vain—his daring axe he heaves
> Tow'rds the black vein a passage cleaves ;
> Dissever'd by the nitrous blast,
> The stubborn barrier bursts at last.

Further pictures of this " Tartarean world " follow,
with their details explained by John Bell in a series of
notes ; and as the visitors return to their beautiful
estate which is described in conventional and artificial
language, Dalton becomes common-place instead of
original in the lines :

> These are the glories of the mine !
> Creative Commerce, these are thine !

It has been remarked that many of the contributors
to the Anthology copy the Ode of Dryden on the
subject of Saint Cecilia, thus finding an opportunity
to express their musical views. In one volume there
is a group of such poems, to which attention may be
called. Among the authors we find the names of
Thomas Bishop, John Oldham, Thomas Shadwell,
Nicolas Brady, Theophilus Parsons, Thomas Yalden,
Christopher Smart and Bonnel Thornton. A few
quotations from these will be enough to show how an
unfortunate musical Saint can be responsible for
several lines of unintelligent verse.

Nicholas Brady (1659–1726). This gentleman,
better known as a Psalmist than as a Poet, was
educated at Westminster and Christ Church. His
life seems to have been largely spent in the collection
of degrees (B.A. 1682, M.A. 1686, D.D. 1699) and
livings. Finally he attained to a Royal Chaplaincy,
Bell writes of him : " Whilst he was engaged in this
undertaking (i.e. the metrical version of the Psalms)
he retired to Richmond . . . and was invited to
accept the Office of Minister. The whole of his
preferments, which were in very pleasant and eligible
situations, amounted to six-hundred a year. . . .

He was a person of a most obliging, sweet, affable temperament, a polite gentleman, an excellent preacher and a good poet." The order of merit in the last line of this eulogy should be noticed.

We learn from his effusion on Saint Cecilia, that the Organ is—

> Brisk without lightness, without dulness grave,
>   Wondrous machine !
> To thee the warbling lute,
> Though us'd to conquest, must be forc'd to yield :
>   With thee unable to dispute
>   The airy violin
>   And lofty viol quit the field ;
>   In vain they tune their speaking strings
> To court the cruel Fair, or praise victorious Kings.

And at the close of the 'Ode,' the heroine becomes an entire orchestra in herself :

> Let these among themselves contest
> Which can discharge its single duty best,
> Thou summ'st their differing graces up in one,
> And art a concert of them all within thyself alone.

Finally, the poet addresses her :

> Hail ! bright Cecilia, hail to thee !
> Great Patroness of Us and Harmony !

But Bishop (*circa* 1680) goes even further. Not content with praising the Organ, he transfers it bodily to heaven to accompany the lady in her celestial hymns :

> The sounding organ does aspire
>   With its monopoly
> Of tuneful sounds to pierce the sky
> And join with its own saint in concert in the heavenly choir.

Bonnel Thornton (1724–1768) at least had become tired of this perpetual harping on one theme, and his verses are refreshingly satirical. He heads them, ' On St. Cecilia's Day—Adapted to the Ancient British Music, viz., the Salt-Box, the Jew's-Harp, the Marrow-Bones and Cleavers, the Hum-Strum or Hurdy-Gurdy, etc., as it was performed on June 10th 1763 at Ranelagh.' He writes :

> The meaner melody we scorn,
>   Which vulgar instruments afford ;
> Shrill flute, sharp fiddle, bellowing horn,
>   Rumbling basoon, or tinkling harpsichord.

> In strains more exalted the salt-box shall join,
> And clattering, and battering, and clapping combine,
> With a rap and a tap, while the hollow side sounds,
> Up and down leaps the flat, and with rattling rebounds

and ends with the following ' Air ' :

> With dead, dull, doleful, heavy hum,
>   With mournful moans,
>   And grievous groans,
> The sober hurdy-gurdy thrums.

Visits, visions, politics, gardens, coal-mines, musical festivals—what a strange gathering of subjects ! Nor does this end the catholic collection of Mr. John Bell. There are ' Epistles ' on Literary Criticism, the Drama, Poetry and on Art ; ' Elegies ' on forlorn ladies and personified virtues ; ' Odes ' on Birthdays, and on historical events such as ' The Spanish Succession ' by a certain Samuel Cobb ; and on trivial themes, such as ' On Breaking a China Quart Mug belonging to the Society of Lincoln College, Oxford,' by an

Undergraduate ; or ' On a Fly that flew into a Lady's
Eye and there lay buried in a Tear.'   These last are
remarkable poetry.   The Oxford Student writes :

> When'er the cruel hand of Death
> Untimely stops a fav'rite's breath,
> Muses in plaintive numbers tell
> How lov'd he lived—how mourn'd he fell :
> Catullus wail his sparrow's fate,
> And Gray immortalise his cat.
> Thrice tuneful Bards ! could I but chime so clever,
> My Quart, my honest Quart, should live for ever !

But R. Fletcher, whoever he may have been, is
even more pathetic :

> Poor envious Soul ! what could'st thou see
> In that bright orb of Purity—
> That active globe—that twinkling sphere
> Of beauty—to be meddling there ?
>
> An amber drop, distilled by
> The sparkling limbec of the eye
> Shall dazzle all the short essays
> Of rubbish worth, and shallow praise.

As might be expected in an anthology of this kind,
there are several anonymous verses of which a few may
be mentioned.   We have ' The Rural Reflections of
a Welch Poet ' in a tripping metre which suits its
subject :

> Stop, stop, my steed ! hail, Cambria, hail,
> With craggy cliffs and darksome vale,
>   May no rude steps defile 'em !
> Your poet, with a vengeance sent
> From London, post, is hither bent,
>   To find a safe asylum.

> Bar, bar the doors, exclude e'en Fear,
> Who press'd upon my horse's rear
>   And made the fleet still fleeter ;
> Here shall my hurried soul repose,
> And, undisturb'd by Irish prose,
>   Renew my lyric metre.

A bold author this, and one who believes that discretion is the better part of valour :

> Ah, since my fear has forc'd me hither,
> I feel no more that sweet blue weather
>   The Muses most delight in ;
> Dark and more dark each cloud impends,
> And ev'ry message from my friends
>   Conveys sad hints of fighting,

and that the peaceful denizens of the country-side will transfer him to safety :

> To harmless themes I'll tune my reed,
> Listen, ye lambkins, whilst you feed,
>   Ye shepherds, nymphs and fountains !
> Ye bees with soporif'rous hums,
> Ye pendent goats, if Hussey comes,
>   Convey me to your mountains.

What he and Hussey had quarrelled about does not appear. Then there are the lines on ' Lord Edge-cumbe's Pig.':

> Hail Pig ! at Tunbridge born and bred
>   Who singlest out his lordship there,
> Event that round the region spread,
>   And made the gaping million stare ;
> And strange it was to see, upon my word,
> A pig for ever trotting with my Lord.

> And some as sagely as the rest
>   Who firm believ'd in transmigrations,
> Pronounc'd this friendly grunting beast
>   One of his Lordship's near relations ;
> Doom'd by the Fates for certain deeds divine,
> To animate the body of a swine !

And those on the good ship " Canterbury " :

> The scaly natives of the deep
>   Press to admire the vast machine,
> In sporting gambols round it leap,
> Or swimming low, due distance keep,
>   In homage to their queen.

Before endeavouring to find some lines which really merit the title of poetry in this collection of artificial jewels, one more effusion must be mentioned, for it is, perhaps, the most perfect example of bathos. In an ' Epistle ' from Soame Jenyns (1704–1787) in the country to Lord Lovelace in London, the writer invites his noble friend to visit him in his pastoral retreat, which is described at length, promising—

> Here you'll be ever sure to meet
> A hearty welcome, though no treat,
> One who has nothing else to do,
> But to divert himself and you :
> A house where quiet guards the door,
> No rural wits smoak, drink and roar ;
> Choice books, safe horses, wholesome liquor,
> Clean girls, backgammon—and the vicar !

Could anyone refuse such lavish hospitality ?

As might be expected in a collection of this kind there are many imitations of Gray's famous ' Elegy,' some of which attain much of its subtle charm. John Langhorne (1735–1779), the translator of Plutarch's Lives, has these melodious lines :

Nor seldom, loitering as I muse along,
  Mark from what flower the breeze its sweetness bore ;
Or listen to the labour-soothing song
  Of bees that range the thymy uplands o'er,

Slow let me climb the mountain's airy brow,
  The green height gain'd, in museful rapture lie.
Sleep to the murmur of the woods below,
  Or look on Nature with a lover's eye.

Another poet laments inevitable death :

Ah, what avails all sublunary state !
  The transient pomp and pageant of a day ;
Since kings and peasants, fellow-slaves of fate,
  When the dread summons comes, must all obey.

Nor lists dull Death to the melodious lyre,
  Nor heeds the raptur'd poet's heavenly song ;
Quench'd in the dust is Milton's muse of fire,
  And mute is Dryden's once harmonious tongue.

John Scott (1730–1783), a Quaker poet who, according
to Bell, " was much respected for his liberality and
beloved for his worth," voices the faith in immortality,
writing of those for whom—

Blows not a flow'ret in th' enamel'd vale,
  Shines not a pebble where the riv'let strays ;
Sports not an insect on the spicy gale,
  But claims their wonder and excites their praise.

For them ev'n vernal nature looks more gay,
  For them more lively hues the fields adorn ;
To them more fair the fairest smile of day,
  To them more sweet the sweetest breath of morn.

They feel the bliss that hope and faith supply :
  They pass serene th' appointed hours that bring
The day that wafts them to the realms on high,
  The day that centers in eternal spring.

Among the simpler and less artificial poems in this anthology may be found ' A Birth-day Offering to a Young Lady from her Lover ' by George Canning, a namesake of the well-known politician, but of whose life little is known, which concludes with the following quaint lines :

When Age her dimpled cheek beguiles
And wrinkles plants instead of smiles ;
When steady to his barbarous plan
To spoil my lovely Mary Anne ;
The savage, unrelenting creature
Has robb'd her face of every feature,
And, to conceptions merely common,
My charmer seems a plain old woman—
Still in my heart she'll hold her throne,
Still in my eyes be twenty-one !

and the better known verses by Nathaniel Cotton (1705–1788), entitled ' The Fire-Side,' with their pleasing final stanza :

Thus hand in hand through life we'll go,
Its checker'd paths of joy or woe
    With cautious steps we'll tread.
Quit its vain scenes without a tear,
Without a trouble or a fear,
    And mingle with the dead.

Time does not permit further excursions into this fascinating collection of ' Fugitive Poetry ' ; but I may, perhaps, conclude with the quotation of a lyric which has the grace and delicacy of the work of a modern poet who was a lover of the eighteenth century. Is there not something akin to the light touch of Austin Dobson in these lines by a poetess of the period ?

" THE BULLFINCH IN TOWN."

Hark to the blackbird's pleasing note,
  Sweet usher of the vocal throng !
Nature directs his warbling throat
  And all that hear admire the song.

Yon bullfinch, with unvary'd tone
  Of cadence harsh and accent shrill,
Has brighter plumage to atone
  For want of harmony and skill.

And while, to please some courtly fair,
  He one dull tune with labour learns,
A well-gilt cage, remote from air,
  And faded plumes is all he earns !

Go hapless captive ! still repeat
  The sounds which Nature never taught—
Go list'ning fair ! and call them sweet,
  Because you know them dearly bought.

Unenvy'd both ! Go hear and sing
  Your studied music o'er and o'er ;
Whilst I attend th' inviting Spring
  In fields where birds unfetter'd soar !

Lady Luxborough.

THE EFFECT OF SCIENTIFIC THOUGHT ON THE ARTS AND LITERATURE.

By Dr. Percy E. Spielmann, B.Sc., F.I.C., F.R.S.L.

[Read February 1st, 1939.]

All forms of Art, using the word in its widest sense, have, for some years past, been showing a vigorous tendency to break away, with revolutionary completeness, from the traditional forms. I do not mean that we can speak of Art as having, at this moment, become suddenly and completely changed ; but that we must realize that there is a vociferous minority that claims to be the spear-head of a development that is to spread continuously and completely. The opposition to this erosion of tradition is made clear by the thousands of visitors that pour into the summer and winter exhibitions of the Royal Academy. Whether the growing generation, nurtured on aeroplanes in place of barouches and wireless communication in place of semaphores, will take to the new movement naturally is an uncomfortable doubt of the moment—but, I feel sure, only for the moment—because the love of beauty is instinctive and fundamental in human nature.

I must here interpolate a comment on the word " development," which I have used only as being nearest to my meaning. Truly, " development " means a gradual expansion of the present towards the future, based on the past ; but in the present case there has been a complete dissociation of modern ideas and standards from those previously accepted. Therefore, the ordinary understanding of the word " development " can only hold here in the sense that the past has been considered, and that the future has been brought upon us in a manner that has been quick and catastrophic, so far as it has gone.

The fundamental difficulty in discussing such matters lies in the absence of a satisfactory answer to the question, What is Art ? From classical times onwards this has been discussed and definitions have been attempted, but there has been no agreement. For the present purpose of giving a basis for consideration as to whether the modern manifestations are " art " the following may be suggested : *Art is the expression or record of reality, an idea or an emotion, produced with skill through an exceptional mind.* This covers all forms of art—painting, sculpture, poetry and the rest.

Another difficulty is that of finding a clear exposition of the aims of Modern Art. Too frequently the explanations that are put before us are so incomprehensible as to raise the suspicion that the Public is being intentionally befogged ; or that the question is being begged because the writer is incompetent to deal with it, and, therefore, can only skirt round it. Amongst the best explanations are the essays in ' Circle ' (1937), and the writings of Herbert Read and Michael Roberts on the side of the progressives, and of Harold Speed and the little journal ' Art and Reason ' on that of traditionalists.

The main underlying cause for the abandonment of tradition is that current art of any branch, to be honest, must be a reflection of the life of the time. Victorian prosperity, serenity, and sentimentality were represented to the full in all the Arts of that epoch.   The War produced a tempestuous and revolutionary period, which in turn produced a tempestuous and revolutionary Art. Mind and nerves were excited ; violent action was associated with violent colouring and edgy, squealing music. Truly, the movement began before the War, when science was becoming a household pet ; but it received its main stimulus during it and afterwards. Edith Sitwell has described this in her nervous, brilliant prose : " If you ask why rhythms have become more violent, the answer is : that this is an age of machinery—a wild race for time, confined within limits that are at once mad and circumscribed. Try to get out and you knock your head against the walls of materialism. This state of things is mirrored in modern syncopated dance music, which removes music from the world of inspiration, which evolves itself organically from the inner need of the artist, and brings it into the world of machinery where form is superimposed as a logical idea.   There is no time or space in which to dream." And yet, however much we may admire and feel peacefully at home with, say, Queen Anne and Georgian architecture, we cannot help realizing that the hideosities of steel and concrete that are allowed to mar even our country-side do more nearly represent the state of society to-day—a society dominated by the great god Efficiency.

Another reason for the change and one which, in my

opinion, justifies change (but not in the crashing degree that we are discussing) lies in the recognition that the production of art along accepted lines has been worked out, and no possibility remains for original work—everything now is more or less a copy of everything else, because it has been done so often before. However stalwart an upholder one may be, as I am, of the Royal Academy and all the stability of beauty in art that it stands for, one cannot help realizing that year after year we are looking at the same unchanging landscapes, subject pictures, and the rest, which we are delighted to see but which, it must be realized, are leading the artist to do nothing more than to repeat the past and even himself. Not only this, but he is usually repeating the past with considerably less excellence than the older artists showed. Who, to-day, can paint flowers as well as the Seventeenth Century Dutch? We exclaim with delight at even a good copy of the style and the beauty of an old Flemish portrait. In recent years, even on the walls of the Royal Academy, few painters have preserved this tradition of the beauty of careful craftsmanship; and it is a reflection of the hurry of this mechanical age that this is so. At the same time, it has been said that, in these days, photography has taken over the duties of representation, leaving the artist free from such demands, so that he may express his inner thoughts and the inner essence of the object or idea that is fermenting in his mind. This view seems to ignore the fact that a representational picture can be just as much a personal production of the artist as any other, and that it takes a necessary place in our world as a true and accurate record, which can show far more than any photograph. Accuracy and art are not mutually destructive.

The only remaining chance for the traditional artist to get away from this canalized condition has been by relying more and more on his personality to give character to his picture. Modern conditions, ranging from psychology to American song writers, have laid heavy stress on this " personality," and modern art is now showing the maximum of personality with the minimum of art—as we normally understand it. And it is amusing to note that this word takes on a most significant meaning for us if it be pronounced as some Americans would pronounce it—" poisonality."

The main object of this paper is to discuss, not the reason for the break-away, but the reason why it has resulted in the particular freakishness that is to be found in the manifestations of the various arts. This, I feel sure, has resulted from science having become a commonplace in our daily lives. It has supplied a stimulating and adventurous inquiry of a new kind into all our affairs ; and has provided the tool of logical thought for criticizing all details of our personal knowledge and practice, of a type that is no longer associated solely with the lecture room and the laboratory. Just as the details of Victorian life have been so sternly called into question by the younger generation to-day, and have been so ruthlessly pruned, so also the tenets of all forms of art have been subjected to the same kind of inquiry with the unemotional attitude that science always requires. That is all to the good, but when scientific conceptions are applied—misapplied I am trying to show—to the *roots* of art, and also to the fountains of its *expression* (as apart from technique), uncouth results are produced.

The present discussion is not concerned with those several artists known to be mad, and the many borderland minds recognized by alienists as being such. But it is interesting just to remember that when Dr. Hyslop, who died a few years ago, and who was for years Senior Physician of Bethlehem Royal Hospital, saw the Post Impressionist movement at its height, he was quite at home in the gallery ; and in certain cases recognized various stages of mental upset and degeneration shown up in the pictures on the wall as closely resembling those produced by patients in his hospital.

Nor is it concerned with those who try to " get away " with incompetence by exalting it for being " untrained " and " naïf " ; nor with those " get-rich-quick " adepts who empty the pockets of the ignorant rich by plausibility.

It is concerned, rather, with the artistic productions of the minority who honestly try to bring about the progress of their art by the exercise of careful thought, but who, in my opinion, appear to have ill-digested the scientific understanding which they sometimes possess to a high degree, and to have applied their conclusions unjustifiably.

A vast amount of exposition has been published, varying from the single inaccurate statement to serious metaphysical reasoning, to explain the basis for modern developments ; and many serious and at the same time fantastic quotations from the writings of artists to explain their works could be put before you.

When the hitherto mathematical conception of the Fourth Dimension has now become a reality in the form of the Space-Time Continuum ; when Relativity has been accepted ; when you are up against the disconcerting fact that in electronic physics you can define the position or the velocity of the electron, but not both at the same time : when these things happen within the stern limitations of science, it is not surprising that queer things happen outside of it, especially when artistic production, inquiry and judgment are carried out with such matters as their background.

It is by now a platitude of the psychologists—and we are all psychologists nowadays or think we are —that the mind is in two parts: the emotional, deep-seated and of immensely long standing, which is bound up with that still unexplained and powerful inner force, instinct; and the intellectual, of relatively late development. All manifestations and appreciation of art are primarily of emotional origin ; the creation and appreciation of beauty are instinctive also ; the canons of art are the canons of beauty. In ordinary life, a balanced individual uses his intellect as a guide and controller of his emotions—" the head controls the heart " in everyday parlance.

In the realm of traditional art—more clearly exemplified by *pictorial art*—the mind is employed for judgment, criticism, and guidance as regards the necessary ingredients of a picture—drawing, colour, composition.   It is also required for the knowledge of technique—compatible and incompatible pigments, the quality and behaviour of vehicles and varnishes, and so on ; the method of applying these to canvas and paper to produce the effect that the artist wishes.

Thus, there is an emotion-to-emotion contact between the artistic creator and the percipient, while intellect stands aside as an observer and guide ; like oil floating on water, intellect and emotion have remained separate, but with an area of contact that is in accord with the nature of each. The most perfect example of this is in the work of Leonardo da Vinci.

But now—and here is the suggested explanation of modern freakishness—the artist has learned, or mis-learned, about the *intellectually*-conceived modern scientific advance and has tried to incorporate it intimately and fundamentally into his *emotionally*-conceived creations, as well as into the expression of those creations ; he has tried to mix his oil and water and gets that queer result, the emulsion.

The chief, though not the first, creator of art to tamper intellectually with the sources of artistic production was Wagner when he developed the " leit-motif." Here, a straightforward and expressive musical production had a kind of fourth dimension added to it, whereby the thoughts of the character were communicated to the audience at the same moment that the orchestra and voice were developing the main situation.

In painting, the Impressionist learned that light can be broken up into spectral colours and be re-combined to form white light ; so he paints in tiny dots or dashes of colour, in the vain expectation that the eye would re-combine them into the effect of sunlight. He does not realize that they do not do so in the ordinary condition of viewing a picture through a normal eye, because the dots are many millions of times coarser than the wave-lengths of light that do so re-combine in a satisfactory manner. But he never seems to learn that to achieve the effect he aims at, the observer must stand so far from the picture that it becomes indefinite through reduction in size.

Also, he learns that crystals can grow in size in suitable conditions and thinks, as some other people do, that they are in some way alive ; so he tries to express the abstract essence of "living" things in geometrical form ; hence the Cubists.

He also violates the mind by trying at the same time to portray the outside and inside of things, simultaneously. Here again is an outrageous and perverted intimate association of science with art, in that the artist actually seeks justification by quoting the behaviour of X-rays : X-rays allow the inside of an opaque object to be made apparent, so why not apply this phenomenon to artistic conceptions ? It is axiomatic that there is only One Truth—a fact or idea cannot be true in one branch of human activity, and be untrue in another. Therefore, he presumably argues, if X-rays are scientific facts, why shouldn't their effects be applied to other branches of human life, such as art ? A strictly logical answer is difficult ; we have to fall back on demanding suitability of application of such principles, and this is a matter of opinion, a thing that can never be absolute.

In addition to these artistic theorists, the Futurists assumed responsibility for shifting the pictorial viewpoint of their pictures, and of using more than one at the same time.

Again, the modern artist is told that Nature is not a collection of individual and independent facts and entities, but that these all are united to form one great Pattern of the Universe, so that he finds justification for concentrating upon and so exaggerating "pattern" in his pictures, that he sacrifices good drawing to this, and so feels justified in painting misshapen objects in unnatural colours on a table or floor of impossible perspective.

Another phase—and this is by far the most important—is the striving after the presentation of the "abstract" by material means. Hampered, as he considers himself to be, by the necessity of always *representing* things as they are seen, the artist now tries to get behind this, and to give the "content" of the subject. There is here some slight affinity, superficial perhaps, with the primitive painters who purposely minimized the outer human representation of the Holy Ones in order to emphasize the religious content of their pictures. But the modernist artist carries the principle so far as to abandon external reality in his striving for extreme simplification. He may consider himself justified in this by having heard that scientific advance, for all its accumulated detail, ever tends to greater simplification of ideas concerning the universe and its contents. He sometimes goes to the extreme limit, when he substitutes completely intellectual conceptions for artistic emotion, and only uses the ordinary materials of the painter and sculptor for demonstrating his ideas, because they are the only ones available, and sometimes he even breaks away from these. When you go from reality to abstraction, you go from the physical to the metaphysical ; and when you try to depict the metaphysical by the physical means of paint, pencil, and paper, something queer is bound to result.   And further, when you remember that traditional art is based on the employment of two accepted illusions—the use of light and shade and of perspective—to represent a three-dimensional world on a two-dimensional surface; then, the use of the two-dimensional surface and of material substances to represent Inside-Outside and the abstract conceptions claimed to be separable from reality, all this is on the direct road to that confused state of the artistic world at which we seem already to have arrived.

This may be seen at any exhibition of modern art. Herbert Read, in his essay, ' The Faculty of Abstraction ' (' Circle ') writes : " Just as surrealism makes use of, or rather proceeds on the assumption of, the knowledge embodied in psycho-analysis, so abstract art makes use of, or proceeds on the basis of, the abstract concepts of physics and dynamics, geometry and mathematics.   It is not necessary for the abstract artist to have a knowledge of these sciences (nor is it necessary for the surrealist to have a knowledge of psycho-analysis) ; such concepts are part of our mental ambience, and the artist is precisely the individual who can make this ambience actual."   Here we find a full acknowledgment of the intellect disturbing the emotional fountains of creation.   We see the controller of the machine becoming part of the machine itself—an impossible condition producing impossible results.   There is here a startlingly close analogy with Communistic political principles.

In *sculpture* the same thing occurs.   The sculptor

also wishes to be free from representing things, and to get to the " content," as he calls it, that underlying abstraction which he considers to be the essence of art.   On that basis he takes joy for their own sake, in the subtle gradations of curvature and the associated play of light, and in relationship of line ; all non-representational.

J. D. Bernal, in his essay, ' Art and the Scientist ' (in ' Circle,' 1937) makes this clear in these words : " Here again, classical art was limited to a small number of curves and surfaces, circles, wave forms, spheres and cylinders.   Modern art has evolved many more subtle forms, especially sculpture, which now depends on far more complex forms and surfaces. .   .   . Originally surfaces are chosen as presenting the most easily executed representation of a natural surface, the dome of a head, or the curve of a torso. In this nature is always pulling back, and tends in the end to destroy the original simplicity in accurate but insignificant detail.   By becoming abstract these restrictions are removed and the study of forms by themselves, moved only by subconscious strivings to representation, can be developed.   At a later stage the two may come together again in a realism informed by the previous analytical study."

But in the same essay Bernal falls into an illogical position.   Dealing with sculpture and its expression through curved surfaces, he cites the contact between the artist and the mathematician, as exemplified in two juxtaposed, slightly-pointed, egg-like bodies, of different sizes, described as " Equi-potential Surfaces of Two Like Charges."   The electrician recognizes these as a valuable lecture-table model : they are, in fact, closely representational—and should be anathema to the modernist sculptural school.

Much the same has been expressed in ' Modern German Art,' by Peter Thoene (p. 67) : " To-day we are breaking up the chaste, ever deceptive phenomena of Nature and reassembling them according to our will. We look through matter, and the day is not far distant when we shall be able to cleave through her oscillating mass as if it were air. Matter is something which man still, at most, tolerates, but does not recognize."

A still further step in the removal of realism away from real things leads to a definite entrance of mysticism (p. 68) : " I have looked at a chair and seen how it hates standing ; its purpose conceals not its beauty, but the curse which lies on it and its fate. Everything is constraint and bondage. It is not true that the chair stands ; it is held ; otherwise it would fly away and unite with the spirit."

Such is the agony of the artistic soul when it is tugged at by the conception of gravity, and further progress in the development of the underlying and fundamental principles of art on these lines will lead to a field of mental activities that is not taken seriously, only sadly.

Again, regarding this matter of representation *versus* abstraction, the modern sculptor would say : " Yes, I see the wonderful rhythm and movement in the draperies of the Elgin marbles, but it is the rhythm that I am interested in, dissociated from the representational realism of the draperies," and he will use their lines and curves having no meaning in themselves, but satisfying to him through his juxtaposition of them. This is why the interested onlooker, trying to understand the mass of stone or wood exhibited before him, is often hampered by the object having some vague resemblance to the form of a known object, usually that of a woman. The explanation of this is that the artist has borrowed the curves from a woman's body, and has then modified them for use in his own way, and the result is primarily a study of curved lines and surfaces of which the source is of minor or of no importance to him, but puzzlingly reminiscent to the onlooker.

There seems, in all this, to be considerable similarity in mentality and aim—indeed, a startlingly close similarity—with those of the medieval alchemists. These inquirers tried to separate the properties of substances from the substances themselves. Quoting from Redgrove's book : "And so the alchemist taught that for the achievement of the *magnum opus* we must strip the metals of their outer properties to develop the essence within." And the alchemists were gropers, exploring an unknown world, on a faulty basis, and making startling accidental discoveries which they didn't (because they couldn't) understand.

There is another aspect of the sculptor's art that shows that intellectual theories are upsetting artistic results. Theoretical argument has led to justification, in the sculptor's eyes, of the production of portrait busts having a surface so flaky as to suggest disease. A doctor friend was asked to go to a certain exhibition and tell me what skin disease all the models were suffering from. With equally straight face he diagnosed " ichthyosis." The alleged justification for this technique lies in another piece of intellectualism again interfering fundamentally with our sense of beauty, and it is this : that you must not completely dominate your medium ; you must allow it to express its individuality. Because a clay bust is built up of flakes of clay, a flaky surface must be left, out of respect for the clay. It is an accepted artistic tenet that a statue, produced in clay to be cast in metal, must not have the look of a marble statue which is produced by chipping. But a competent sculptor can show this by his general treatment of the subject, and it does not need such queer reasoning and non-natural means to express it. We can appreciate Barry Pain's approval of all that the founder of a school had done, except the school.

The same break with tradition is to be observed in *architecture*, but it is not possible to interpret this along the lines of my thesis, because two influences obscure it. Firstly, the recent development of steel and concrete has imposed such imperious engineering influences on the created building that any intellectual-artistic interplay, such as I have been discussing, is swamped. Secondly, any activities in the world of architecture, indulged in as freely as those on canvas or in stone, would be severely curbed by the local authority dealing in matters of health and safety and local amenities.

The same thing is happening in *music* : civilization is being reflected. In the period of placid Victorian prosperity we most characteristically had Mendelssohn; to-day, music is reflecting the machine shop. Such music of roaring rhythm has an amazingly exciting effect whether one is a civilized being or an African native, and of the kind experienced in much less degree with military music. Otherwise modern music has ceased to have a purely emotional basis, developed and shepherded by the intellect's watchfulness, and for more than one reason.

A new chord has been discovered, which so far sounds cacophonous to many of us, but which is useful in providing the composer with a means of modulating between a larger number of keys than before. But more recently tonality has gone. Instruments in a quartet may each play in a different key. Music has become synthetic; it is called " blackboard music," and takes its place shoulder to shoulder with a game of chess.

The use of the mind in directing the most beautiful employment of words to express the emotion of the *poet*, has given way to the intellectual conception of using words as though they were individuals having an independence of their own. The mathematician, C. L. Dodgson, more widely beloved as " Lewis Carroll," tried to use words as though they were mathematical symbols and with analogous significance; but he, wisely, was content to remain whimsical.

The fusion of mathematical concepts into poetry is to-day made very clear by Ezra Pound, in a statement quoted by Michael Roberts in his ' Critique of Poetry ' (p. 84) : " Poetry is a sort of inspired mathematics, which gives equations, not for abstract figures, triangles, spheres, and the like, but equations for human emotions." It is highly significant that such ideas should enter a poet's mind at all, whatever the degree of use that may be made of them.

Many modern poems have little or no meaning according to the usual understanding to be given to the words or sentences : at best they consist of a sort of tessellated pavement of words, sometimes invented, giving a barely recognizable significance. Babette Deutsch (in 'This Modern Poetry,' 1936, p. 25) states : "It is perhaps inevitable that the vocabulary of the modern poet should need elucidation. With the increasing specialization of knowledge, he is apt to use the idiom of his special field of interest: astronomy, scholasticism, geology, physics—an idiom which an audience unfamiliar with it may regard as mere pedantry. If he uses words not only for their symbolic connotations, but for the multiple meanings provided by the pun, he erects so many more hurdles for the reader to leap. Before education became popular, the poet wrote for his intellectual equals. To-day, aware that the circle of those who will understand all his references is limited, he is apt to offend the general by addressing his peers in the key-phrases, the elliptical diction that we all use in commerce with our intimates, and of salting his verse with private jokes. His readiness to try every rhythmic invention is matched by his interest in all the resources of language, including specific jargons and dialects, and neologisms of his own making."

This seems to me to be an excellent summary of the modern poet's attitude of mind and his tampering with his sources of inspiration ; and most significant is the emphasis on " interest " and not a hint about beauty. This can be applied directly to the prose of James Joyce and the work of Harry Crosby. In 'Anna Livia Plurabelle,' about one-third of the words used are of the author's invention ; in a poem by the latter all the words are completely new, completely incomprehensible, and many unpronounceable. This separation of a word from any meaning evidently links with the " abstract-making " mentality of the artist that attaches more importance to the curve than to the body from which it was taken, and also connects with the alchemists who tried to separate the properties of matter from matter itself. At the same time, poetry has become so " free " as to be practically indistinguishable from prose. It is remarkable that, in so doing, there has been a complete loss of that rhythm which has always been so essential to traditional poetry, and which is to-day so heavily insisted upon and so painfully sought for, in the sister arts of painting and sculpture.

It has been said that the downfall of poetry began with the printing press of Caxton, because from that moment, the knowledge of poetry increased immensely, and at the same time ceased to appeal to the ear alone, and began to appeal to the eye. A halfway house has been, perhaps, the recognition of " eye-rhymes." To-day the change of appeal is complete. Much characteristic modern poetry cannot be taken in by the ear alone, because it must be seen with the eye so that the full effect may be attained through the frequently extraordinary typesetting. Such adventitious effect was also anticipated by " Lewis Carroll " in his poem about the Mouse's Tail. Much of it consists of " image pattern," a poem in which the words employed do not give comprehensible sentences, but act as individuals to arouse a series of images in the mind—that is receptive to them. It is significant that the word " pattern " crops up again.

Having surveyed, and in some degree analysed, the various sections of my theme, there remains to be considered briefly the basic mental attitude of the practitioners in its broadest aspect.

Accepting as genuine the serious enthusiasm that they express for the new theories that are being put into practice, how is it possible that such strange productions are welcomed with such real delight and admiration ?

The answer lies in the attention that is being increasingly paid to the developing science of psychology. I say " developing," as this subject is so difficult, so elusive, so specialized in its methods of research and interpretation, and, as compared with the other sciences, so young that it has not yet reached the stage of being an established science like chemistry and geology.

It has, however, reached the state of progress when its results are sufficiently definite to be considered and discussed and tested in all directions of human activities.

Just as psychology gets behind the realism of our everyday thoughts and actions, so modern artistic theory purports, with its aid, to get behind the realities of traditional artistic thought and production. Just as cause is linked inevitably to effect, and is urgently sought and studied in order to understand effect, so the cause behind our mental activities is being examined intensively for the same purpose.

This has led to the discovery in the individual of complexes and mental states which, being biological, are to some degree indefinite and mercurial ; and further research will doubtless diminish this. But for the time being, great importance is put by its discoverer on anything that is fished up from the unconscious mind for examination by the conscious, even though it may be of an unsavoury nature. And whatever these new discoveries may be, the revelation to him of his mental state so fascinates the Poet and prose writer that he must " tell the world " about it, in place of singing the older beauties.

But he finds that he can only do this by some indirect method such as reiteration and word-symbols. Communication from his mind to that of his reader is to-day undisciplined by the older technical limits of rational thought and modes of expression, or indeed by any form of restraint ; so that restrictions being down, the road is open to that mental jungle which we find occasionally already being presented to us.

To sum up : We realize that the arts have been changing in consonance with the change in world conditions, and that this was accelerated by the War. We see that the direction of this change has been controlled by the unjustifiable application of scientific theory to the roots of artistic creation.

The result has been that artistic expression has been intellectualized at its fount, with loss of beauty and emotion ; and that the word " art " has been given, suddenly and almost explosively, a new connotation.

At the same time, a general loosening of restraint, noticeable in all our social relations, has removed any reticence in the public expression of such developments.

Enjoyment to-day is no longer a matter of quiet contemplation of beautiful things for their own sakes ; it consists of a tenser kind of thing—the joy of intellectual stimulation. Thus, beauty is to disappear from life, if we listen to the new prophets of art. But having listened to them we will pass them by, because the far deeper instinct of man for beauty tells us *that they are false prophets.* As C. F. A. Voysey, the famous architect, says : " What liars these people are, who falsify beauty ! ".

DOCTRINE OF HUMAN PERSONALITY IN IQBAL'S POETRY.

By A. YUSUF ALI, C.B.E., F.R.S.L.

[Read November 9th, 1938.]

POET-PHILOSOPHERS are more usual in the East than in the West. But may we say that the trend of modern post-War poetry in the West also is in the direction of philosophizing ? Is not Eliot a mystic, and Auden a singer of " a turning globe," which " has thrust us up together " ?

However that may be, certainly the two greatest poets of modern India are philosophers. Rabindranath Tagore represents the contemplative, devotional, *Bhakti* philosophy of Vaishnava Hinduism. Take passages like the following :—

> " Dream is a wife who must talk,
> Sleep is a husband who silently suffers."
> *(Stray Birds*, 118.)

" I carry in my world that flourishes the worlds that have failed."—*(Stray Birds*, 121.)

Their haunting poetic beauty, their epigrammatic terseness, yet sum up a whole inner world of human Personality, about whose truth or application philosophers will dispute to the end of time.

Iqbal's world is no less subtle, but it is altogether different, both in tone and tempo, in the source of its inspiration and in the struggle which it seeks to incite

in his readers. Courage, Power, Action are the
Ideals he would point to. Swiftness, forcefulness,
unflinching assertion of Personality are the watch-
words which he would din into the ears of a lethargic
world. He says :

" Endeavour to surge and wrestle with the sea . . .
   Oh, expand thyself ! Move swiftly !
   Be a cloud that shoots lightning and sheds a flood of rain !
   Let the ocean sue for thy storms as a beggar,
   Let it complain of the straitness of thy skirts ! "
(A.K.,* 1309–1316.)

The source of his inspiration is the Qur-ān and
the religious and poetic traditions of Islam in its most
vigorous days. In form and substance he has based
himself on Maulāna Jalāl-ud-din Rūmī, whose volu-
minous ' mathnavi ' is one of the treasures of Persian
literature, indeed of the world's literature. But
Iqbal is also steeped in modern philosophy, not as a
follower but as a critic,—one might almost say, as a
fierce assailant of its conclusions. His denunciations
of Plato show little sympathy with that philosopher,
and—I hesitate to say it—little understanding of his
philosophy or of its influence on early Islamic thought.
Nietzsche and Karl Marx are referred to, but on the
whole they are rejected as smacking of Western
materialism. A number of modern names are drawn
upon to illustrate the arguments. Eastern names,
like those of Jamāl-ud-dīn Afghāni and Halīm Pasha
serve to illustrate the idea of the universal non-
national, non-racial Society of Islam, while Western

* A. K., or for shortness, A. = *Asrar i Khudī*. For this work I have
generally quoted Dr. R. A. Nicholson's translation, and the figures refer
to the lines in that translation.

names, such as that of Kitchener, are used to illustrate Western Imperialism.   The League of Nations
is described in these extraordinary terms: "A few
grave-clothes-snatchers have made an association for
the division of graves (among themselves) " : (*Kafan-
duzdé chand bahr i taqsīm i qubūr anjumane sakhta and*).
I do not know how far the most rabid enemies of the
League would recognize their *bête noire* in that cari-
cature.   The most usual indictment of the League is
that it is a model of utter idealistic futility.

In Iqbal's world we are to seek struggle and tension,
not peace and calm.   Life, to use his own words in
illustration of his poetical philosophy, is ever " a
forward assimilative movement."   Personality is " a
state of Tension," and it is the state of tension that
" tends to make us immortal."   The struggle which
we should make is to maintain this tension, to absorb
the whole world into ourselves, not to be absorbed.
" Love is the desire to assimilate, to absorb," not to
lose ourselves in the object of our love.   He would
dissent from Tennyson's lines :

> "Love took up the Harp of Life,
>   and smote on all the chords with might,
> Smote the chord of Self that, trembling,
>   passed in music out of sight."

Nor would he approve of the Sūfi ideal, to be lost in
God.   For he uncompromisingly attacks the Sūfi
mystics, especially Hāfiz and Sa'dī, for preaching the
renunciation of the Self in order to reach God.

We must clearly take in the general atmosphere
before we can fully understand Iqbal and his doctrine
of Personality.

A few facts of his outer life may be mentioned.   He was born in 1876, in Sialkot, a border town of the Punjab, about 50 miles from Jammu, the winter capital of Kashmir.   He came of Kashmiri stock, and the Persian language and Persian literature were almost in his blood.   He studied, and afterwards taught, philosophy under the Punjab University.   In 1905 he came to Europe, qualified for the Bar, entered Cambridge, and got a doctorate in philosophy from the Munich University.   Philosophy and poetry do not consort well with practice at the Bar or the rough and tumble of politics.   He neglected the Bar, and his political ambitions were not fulfilled, although he was elected a member of the old Punjab Legislative Council for a term and was nominated for a session of the Round Table Conference in London, which hammered out the new Constitution for India now partially in force.   He was President of the Anjuman i Himayat i Islam, a Muslim educational body in Lahore, for two or three years.   The last years of his life were clouded by illness, which practically kept him in bed.   He died in April, 1938.

Iqbal began to write poetry quite early.   He wrote a number of short pieces in Urdu, which have been collected under the titles of ' Bāng i Darā ' (N.D.), ' Bāl i Jibrīl' (1935), and ' Dharb i Kalīm' (1936).   His fame, however, will rest on the works which he published in Persian.   Among these may be mentioned the following :

1. ' Asrār i Khudi,' ' Secrets of the Self (or the Ego),' published in 1915.   An English translation with a notable Introduction was published

by Prof. R. A. Nicholson, of Cambridge, in 1920. We shall presently discuss this work of Iqbal.

2. ' Rumūz i Be-Khudi,' ' Mysteries of Self-Denial,' a pendant to the ' Asrār.' It develops a philosophy of Society based on the eternal Ummat of Islam.

3. ' Payām i Mashriq,' ' The Message of the East,' a series of poems in imitation of Goethe's ' West-Östlicher Diwan.' It assumes that the West is sunk in materialism and intellectualism, without a goal or purpose, and invites it to look more within.

4. ' Zabūr i 'Ajam,' ' The Psalmody of Persia.' Here a number of philosophical ideas are discussed.   The last two pieces are characteristic. They are entitled ' The Religion of Slaves ' and ' The Art of Building up Free Men.'   A line may be quoted :

" In Slavery Love and Religion are separated :
    The honey of Life becomes nauseous in Taste."

5. ' Jāwīd nāma,' ' The Book of Jāwīd,' that being the name of his youngest son.   This is a mystic Allegory, somewhat in the style of Dante's Divine Comedy, but in an expressly Muslim setting.   There is also in it a reminiscence of some of the Mi'rāj Poems of medieval Islam, which, according to Asin, in some sort suggested the form of Dante's Poem.   In Iqbal's journey through the various heavens of the Solar System and beyond, his guide is the Persian mystic

Jalād ud din Rūmi, and he meets various friends and enemies of Islam, from Abū Jahl the relentless persecutor of the Prophet Muhammad, to Nietzsche the Superman Philosopher, and Farzmarz the extreme and wicked feminist. Each of them talks dramatically, expounding his or her own views. As Nietzsche's doctrine of the Superman and the will to power has many points of contact with Iqbal's ideas but leaves out God, Nietzsche is described as the Root without the Fruit.

In my opinion, the ' Asrār ' and the ' Rumūz,' though they are themselves somewhat loose in texture, present the leading ideas of Iqbal in a connected form, while the other works are variations on similar themes. His English Lectures on the Reconstruction of Religious Thought in Islam are a remarkable contribution : they attempt a statement of Muslim religious philosophy " with due regard to the philosophical traditions of Islam and the more recent developments in the various domains of human knowledge." But our business at present is not with Theology, but with the doctrine of Personality. Before discussing this in detail, I ought to note the leading ideas, which occur again and again in Iqbal's works in different forms, and express as it were the quintessence of his own personality.

He judges everything by the touchstone of Islam, not as expounded by its doctors, ancient or modern, but as understood by Iqbal in its philosophical, social, political, and personal aspects. While taking the great Sūfi Jālal-ud-din Rūmi as his master and guide,

he rails against the Sūfi schools as too other-worldly,
as sapping the strength and virility of Islam.   Against
ascetic Sūfiism in all its forms he wages an unceasing
war.   He considers it to be a form of freethought and
in alliance with Rationalism.*   This dictum can
hardly be accepted as historically true.   On the other
hand, his protest against the exploitation of Sūfiism,
in modern India (and elsewhere) by selfish and ignorant
men is both reasonable and effective, and finds an
echo in a great deal of current literature in India.

The contrast between the East and the West, much
to the spiritual and moral disadvantage of the West,
is almost an obsession in Iqbal.   It colours his views
on many questions, social, political, and economic.   In
this, perhaps, he is expressing the general sentiments
of the educated rising generation in India—and not
in India only, but throughout what we may call the
Near East.   Iqbal delighted in such books as
Spengler's ' Decline of the West.'   He imagined that
thinkers in the West were agreed that the days of the
West were done, and elicited loud applause when he
expressed such sentiments.   Political conditions
explain the paradox that those who have received
western education are, as a class, the bitterest critics
of the West.   Slavery and Freedom, Capitalism and
Socialism or Communism, Materialism and Spirituality,
the Inward Eye and the Worship of the Outer Good,
Imperialism and the Spirit of Submission, Modern-
ism and Wholesome Tradition,—such are some of the
slogans through which the contrast is sought to be
expressed.   Iqbal's ' Dharb i Kalīm ' has a sub-title
on the title-page—' A Declaration of War against the

* ' Reconstruction of Religious Thought,' ed. 1930, p. 211.

Present Age.' In the same book (p. 95) we have the following poem on ' Woman and Education ' :

> " If European civilisation
> Is the death of the Nation,
> Death is its fruit also
> For the Individual Man.
> The education whose influence
> Makes a woman unwomanly,—
> Far-seeing people
> Call such education Death.
> If the schooling of woman
> Is divorced from Religion,
> Then, as regards Love and Affection,
> Knowledge and Art are but Death."

We have thus a strong vein of innate conservatism combined with the most revolutionary doctrines for the Individual and for Society. It is doubtful whether such a combination is either logical, consistent or practicable. Elsewhere I have called Iqbal's philosophy a " mystical protest against mysticism." The form, the tone, the spirit is mystical. The content can only be described as Iqbalism. He is conscious of that. His spirit took a wide sweep. It wandered, as a poet's spirit should, over worlds beyond ken. But all the time he felt he was alone. " In the midst of the Assembly, I am solitary," he cries in the ' Asrār' ("dar miyān i anjuman, tanhā-stam),'* and he repeats the cry towards the end. He has to free himself from Yesterday and To-morrow, and behold another world in his own heart (A. 1550).

To Iqbal the doctrine of Personality is not mere

---

* A. 1655. I have departed from Dr. Nicholson's translation here, as I think greater stress on the loneliness is required by the context. See also A. 1700.

metaphysical speculation.   It is an important secret
vouchsafed to him, to be rehearsed to a sorrowful
world.   He has the urge of a prophet, and he invites
the world to listen and profit by it :

> " Come, if thou wouldst know
> The secret of everlasting life !
> Come, if thou wouldst win
> Both earth and heaven."
>   (A. 69–70.)

What is this Khudī, this Self, this Personality ?

> " My being was
> An unfinished statue,
> Uncomely, worthless,
> Good for nothing.
> Love chiselled me :
> I became a man
> And gained knowledge
> Of the nature of the universe."
>   (A. 151–4).

Seven propositions implicit in Iqbal's argument may
be first stated categorically, and then considered in
detail.   They are : (1) that man, in his unregenerate
state, is but dust ; (2) that there is yet in him a
potentiality, which opens up to him the highest
destiny in the universe ; (3) that the unfolding of
that potentiality is through the Khudi, the Self ; (4)
that that Self or Personality requires to be constantly
exercised and developed through Love ; (5) that the
channel for that development is the Gospel of Tauhīd
or Unity, the mystic personality of Muhammad the
Prophet ; (6) that Intellect, modern knowledge,
common virtues like humility or contentment,—
anything that is " shackled in the senses " (A. 1477–80)

is a mere blind and leads away from Perfection ; and (7) that the Inner Light in the Self is creative ; the pith of Life is action (A. 1019) and strength (A.1067). The Nietzschean tendency is evident, especially in the statement that Life's " mainspring is the desire for victory, and mercy out of season is a coldness of blood " (A. 1046–7). The only difference between Nietzsche and Iqbal is that Iqbal brings in his own idea of religion, of Islam, and of God, as the basis of the whole agreement, while Nietzsche rejects God altogether.

As he frequently refers to Rūmi as his guide, let us glance at Rūmi's idea on the subject of ' Khudi.' The germ of the ' Khudi ' idea can be found in three couplets of Rūmi ; but its growth, development, and conclusions appear to me to be entirely different— almost at opposite poles—from those of Iqbal. Rūmi, towards the end of his ' Mathnavi,' describes three types of men—the wise man, the half-wise man, and the fool. The wise man has personality and light ; the half-wise man learns from him ; the fool learns from nothing. Let me quote from Rūmi :

" The wise man is he who has a torch : he is the guide and leader of the caravan. He goes in the van, following his own Light (*pairawe Nur e Khud ast*) and obeying his own Self, while the others follow other than their Selves. He believes in himself and his faith in the Light on which his soul feeds."* This is the doctrine of the Inner Light or Conscience as illuminated by God. In another place Rūmi says : " Leave power and weakness alone ; whatever withdraws thine eyes from God is an idol " (' Persian

* I translate from the Lahore edition, 1928, vol. iv, p. 232.

Mystics' Rūmi, p. 701, Wisdom of the East).   The Sūfis went on developing this doctrine.   Two centuries after Rūmi, Jāmi wrote in his ' Lawā'ih :

> " Make my heart pure, my soul from error free,
> Make tears and sighs my daily lot to be,
> And lead me on Thy road away from Self,
> That lost to Self I may approach to Thee."
>
> (Whinfield's translation.)

We may observe the remarkable way in which the stream of the Sūfi doctrine of Self has been diverted by Iqbal from its original trend through the intervention of Nietzsche until it runs almost in the opposite direction.

But let us return to Iqbal.   If we only look to man's physical nature, man is no more than clay and water. But, according to Quranic phraseology, God breathed His spirit into him.   He has now, therefore, to become the vicegerent of God in God's Creation.   He has to conquer his body, and let his thought reach to the skies.   There is a danger that mere thought, mere mind, mere intellect may make not-Self appear as the Self.   Therefore the real Self should be strengthened and asserted, even though it may involve pain and anguish to others.   There may be much " wastefulness and cruelty in the shaping and perfecting of spiritual beauty " (A. 205–6).

Rejecting the Buddhist injunction to kill Desire, Iqbal would on the contrary " set Desire dancing in the breast " (A. 275).   Desire enriches life.   " We live by forming ideals ; we glow with the sunbeams of Desire " (A. 321–2).   Desire became Love ;   the highest love is the love of God and His Prophet.   But do not ask or beg. That is weakness. "Pray God for Courage; wrestle with Fortune" (A. 464). "Desire is Love's Message to Beauty" (A. 680), and Beauty creates Desire. Hence arises the Poet's duty to sing of Beauty and fire the hearts of men. Hence the need for a reform of Islamic literature.

How came it that the doctrine of strength and the assertion of self gave place to the doctrine of self-denial and self-negation? The latter was invented by subject-races to weaken the character of rulers and conquerors. The wakeful tiger was thus called to slumber. Poverty and humility were exalted, and strength and independence declined. The decline was called "Moral Culture" (A. 630). The only case in which the Individual should subordinate his personality arises in relation to the ideal Society of Islam, which is expounded in Iqbal's ' *Rumūz.*'

While the Individual must push forward and conquer, he can only do so by obeying the Law of Islam. He must learn self-command and self-control. He must abjure fear. He must give up " love of riches and power, love of country, love of self and kindred and wife" (A. 859–60), because of that higher Love, the love of God and of the Law of Islam. Thus is obtained the divine vicegerency. Such a vicegerent " wakes and sleeps for God alone " (A. 910). He is the perfect Man, the rider of Destiny. " Nature travails in blood for generations, to compose the harmony of his personality" (A. 939–40). The Prophet's cousin 'Ali was such a man.

The Coal in the mine and the Diamond are similar in origin and composition. Yet Coal is held in low esteem, while the Diamond shines in splendour and

becomes " the light of a monarch's eye " (A. 1211).
Why is this ? The Diamond thus explains it to the
Coal :

> " Dark earth, when hardened,
> Becomes in dignity as a jewel.
> Having been at strife
> With its environment,
> It is ripened by the struggle
> And grows hard like a stone.
> 'Tis this ripeness that has endowed
> My form with light
> And filled my bosom
> With radiance.
> Because thy being is immature,
> Thou hast become abased ;
> Because thy body is soft,
> Thou art burnt.
> Be void of fear,
> Grief, and anxiety.
> Be hard as a stone ;
> Be a diamond !
> Whoever strives hard
> And grips tight,
> The two worlds
> Are illumined by him."
>
> (A. 1214–24).

It then comes to this. Personality is power,
striving, the resistance to the presence of outside
circumstances of all kinds. But, as we saw, the Self
is not exempt from the Law of Islam. It is a perfect
Law, an eternal Law, and in itself it makes for strength
and the building-up of the Self. It reconciles the
categories of permanence and change, as the Self in
striving is always developing, expanding, and in
motion. If you understand eternal principles to

exclude all possibilities of change, you produce the immobility which has gripped Islamic peoples for the last 500 years. On the other hand, if you have no eternal principles to regulate your collective life, you go on changing and changing, but you fail, as Europe has done, says Iqbal, in her political and social science.* The law of change and adaptation, subject to eternal principles, being admitted, it is difficult to follow Iqbal's plea that each community should remain attached to itself to follow its ancestral traditions. Even the idol-worshipper need not abandon his idols. If he is a Brahman, he should be worthy of his sacred thread. " O trustee of an ancient culture, turn not away from the ways of thy fathers " (A. 1259–60). This seems to me to be inconsistent both with the Law of Islam (' Qur-ān,' xxi, 52–54 ; ii, 170) and with Iqbal's own philosophy of Life.

The Self, then, is to Iqbal the fundamental fact of the universe. Let Iqbal expound this in his own words :

" All life is individual ; there is no such thing as universal life. God Himself is an individual ; He is the most unique individual. The universe, as Dr. McTaggart says, is an association of individuals ; but we must add that the orderliness and adjustment which we find in this association is not eternally achieved and complete in itself. It is the result of instinctive or conscious effort. We are gradually travelling from chaos to cosmos and are helpers in this achievement."†

* Iqbal, 'Reconstruction of Religious Thought,' ed. 1930, p. 207.
† Iqbal in the Introduction to Dr. Nicholson's ' Asrār,' p. xvii.

There are a few questions that remain unanswered. Is every individual man capable of becoming an *Insān i Kāmil*, a Perfect Man ? What becomes, then, of the Unique Individual ? For in Iqbalian philosophy man is not finally absorbed in God : on the contrary, he absorbs God into himself.* This cannot happen to every individual man as a separate entity. Then, if there is no final cessation of the struggle, this world with its imperfections must be eternal ; but Islam denies this (' Qur-ān,' lv, 26). Again, if for the sake of a single Rose, the Self destroys a hundred rose-gardens (A. 201), or, if the flames of the Self have to burn a hundred Abrahams that the lamp of one Muhammad may be lighted (A. 213–14), what becomes of the souls unsuccessful in the struggle ? And if there are no failures, how can we conceive of millions and millions of perfect ones ? But perfection itself can only be reached when the struggle ceases, just as prophecy, to use Iqbal's own words, " reaches its perfection in discovering the need of its own abolition."† How, then, can the struggle be unceasing ?

Now a word about Iqbal's place in the roll of the Muslim poets of India. The last three-quarters of a century have seen revolutionary changes in Indian Muslim thought. The Indian Muslims had been declining in power as well as original thought for over a century and a half. But the Indian Mutiny marks the definite close of the period of their work as an active striving factor in leadership. After that, three great names stand out pre-eminent among the Muslim

* Iqbal, *ibid.*, p. xix.
† Iqbal, *ibid.*, p. 176.

poets in India, viz. Ghālib, Hāli and Iqbal. Every
one of them wrote in Persian as well as in Urdu. In
Ghālib's time Persian still held the prestige of having
been the all-India official and cultural language, and
his best work is divided in bulk between Persian and
Urdu. Hāli, who published his ' *Musaddas* ' in
1879, undoubtedly did most of his best work in Urdu.
Iqbal's best work has been in Persian, and I have
heard complaints on this score in Urdu circles. While
Ghālib gave a chiselled form to Urdu prose, and Hāli
introduced a more modern form in Urdu verse, both
in style and subject-matter, Iqbal missed a great
chance in neglecting Urdu. He had it in him, with
his English education and his wide interest, both
literary and psychological, in the world at large, to
have carried the modernization of Urdu a stage
farther and enlarged the outlook of his Urdu readers
instead of confirming them in their narrower tendencies. His Persian verse takes its inspiration from
mediaeval classical Persian, which means that he
adheres to the conventions in style and metaphor
which modern Persians are trying to get over.

In texture of thought the three poets stand out
distinct and apart. Ghālib had to face the disastrous
sequels of the social and political revolution which he
so bitterly lamented. But he interpreted the inner
revolution which was less patent to the ordinary
mind. From the note of despair which he sounded,
the Aligarh educational movement aimed at rescuing
the Indian Muslims by directing them to the modern
tendencies of the world at large, which now came from
the West. Hāli was associated with that movement
and with its founder, Sir Saiyid Ahmad Khan. He,

therefore, in reviewing the past found these very tendencies in early Islam, and made an impassioned appeal to his people to adopt them and march forward to progress. In Iqbal's generation the pendulum has swung the other way. Mainly because of political movements, the West was very much out of favour, and Iqbal accentuated that attitude. But he did a real service to his people in calling them back to the more manly virtues of their ancestors. His talent lay in a searching criticism, sometimes carried to extremes, of the false standards of his age. His message was to condemn apathy, timidity, and obscurantism, and put activity, courage and practical achievement in the forefront of his programme. To this end he wrote with the enthusiasm and emotional *élan* of the mystic Sufis whom he condemned. He was after all a mystic in the war which he waged against mysticism. His doctrine of Personality is really a doctrine of activity, with an unbounded field of thought and action in the world of Islam.

GIFF EDMONDS MEMORIAL LECTURE

This Lecture perpetuates the loved memory of Lieutenant Nicholas Gilford Edmonds of the 2nd Black Watch, who was killed at Magersfontein, his first battle, December 11th, 1899. It was founded by his sister, Mrs Sybella Edmonds, a member of this Society since 1918.

LOST MANUSCRIPTS

By Dr. Ronald Knowr

[Read May 31st, 1939.]

In August of the year 1854 Thomas Jefferson Hogg, the friend of Shelley, was writing to Mary daughter of Thomas Love Peacock, then the wife of George Meredith, that anon of a nervous intellectual, with a dyspeptic intellectual, which was destined to end so disastrously. Hogg was an entertaining and discursive letter writer, wandering readily from topic to topic, and in this letter he speaks à propos de bottes of Goethe's Wilhelm Meister.

"I am now reading Wilhelm Meister," he writes, "for the third time, and with increased delight. I used to wish that people would find the lost Decades of Livy or the lost Comedies of Menander, but I had rather now that you should find the unwritten books of Wilhelm Meister. They find them amongst Herculaneum Papyri or Palimpsest MSS. Since you are such a clever girl, pray find them for me; and publish them, so that I may have a new volume every

GIFF EDMONDS MEMORIAL LECTURE.

This Lecture perpetuates the loved memory of Lieutenant Nicholas Gifford Edmonds of the 2nd Black Watch, who was killed at Magersfontein, his first battle, December 11th, 1899. It was founded by his sister, Miss Sophia Edmonds, a member of this Society since 1919.

LOST MANUSCRIPTS.

By Dr. Robin Flower.

[Read May 31st, 1939.]

In August of the year 1854 Thomas Jefferson Hogg, the friend of Shelley, was writing to Mary, daughter of Thomas Love Peacock, then the wife of George Meredith, that union of a nervous intellectual with a dyspeptic intellectual which was destined to end so disastrously. Hogg was an entertaining and discursive letter writer, wandering readily from topic to topic, and in this letter he speaks *à propos de bottes* of Goethe's Wilhelm Meister :

" I am now reading Wilhelm Meister," he writes, " for the third time, and with increased delight. I used to wish that people would find the lost Decades of Livy or the lost Comedies of Menander ; but I had rather now that you should find the unwritten books of Wilhelm Meister. Pray find them amongst Herculanean Papyri or Palimpsest MSS. Since you are such a clever girl pray find them for me ; and publish them, so that I may have a new volume every

two or three months for the rest of my life." From
this letter we may see the kind of lost literature which
a man of some general culture, the friend of Shelley
and Peacock, classical scholars both, hoped to see
recovered in the middle of the last century, and the
sources to which he would look for that revelation.
The dream of the restoration of the lost books of
Livy had haunted the scholars of the Renaissance,
and in our own day an Italian professor has mocked
the learned world with a false claim to this very
discovery. Menander, the master of the New
Comedy, dimly seen through fragments and the
imitations of his Roman pupil, Terence, has at last
come to light in our times, as we shall see, but not
from the source of Hogg's anticipations. Wilhelm
Meister remains as he was and I suppose that, if
further parts of that remarkable work should emerge
from some forgotten German library, few of us would
devote the rest of our lives to their perusal.

The sources of discovery suggested by Hogg are
as characteristic of his period as his desiderata. The
disinterment of the buried cities of Pompeii and Herculaneum in the eighteenth century had raised the
most sanguine hopes. Certain of these hopes have
been justified. The excavations there have shed a
flood of light upon life in a Roman provincial town
of the imperial age, its administration, its business,
its art in sculpture, mosaic and fresco, its amusements
in theatre and arena, and the endless, fascinating
trivialities of its daily life. In literature we have
not been so fortunate. Little in the way of manuscripts has been recovered from Pompeii, unless we
reckon under that heading the business accounts of

the banker, L. Caecilius Jucundus, inscribed upon the wax tablets which the Romans used for the informal purposes of life and literature. Herculaneum has proved more fruitful, possibly because that town was obliterated by a torrent of liquid mud, while Pompeii met its fate under a rain of hot ashes. Here, early in the excavations, a whole library was unearthed, and the rolls of papyrus there discovered have been unrolled with infinite care and scrupulously deciphered. It is a little unfortunate that the literature thus recovered is rather uniform in character, the writings of the philosopher Philodemus and other works of the sect of the Epicureans. What results the further exploration of Herculaneum may hold in store it is impossible to predict, but nothing forbids us to hope for additions to our knowledge of classical literature from this source.

Hogg rests another expectation on the decipherment of palimpsests. He was probably thinking here of Cardinal Mai's famous discovery of the ' De Republica ' of Cicero in a palimpsest in the Vatican. Here again results have been rather disappointing. A palimpsest in the British Museum has restored to us the lost historian Licinianus. But no major work of ancient literature at all comparable to Mai's find has been recovered for us by this means. This is the more unfortunate, as the use of ultra-violet and infra-red light greatly facilitates the reading of these obscured texts in modern times. Here again there is still room for hope in the further exploration of libraries.

But there is one source of discovery, the most fruitful of all in modern times and the one which would most naturally occur to a scholar of our day, which Hogg does not so much as mention, the great and increasing multitude of papyri miraculously preserved in the sands of Egypt which have earned for the last half century the just title of one of the great ages of discovery. The consideration of what our gain has been from this source I will reserve for the moment.

I propose in this lecture to discuss, not so much lost MSS. in themselves as the recovery of MSS. in the past, and the methods which may be employed with good hope to add to these resuscitations in the future. It is certain that the great majority of the MSS. ever written have been lost. Of some of these we have records, but for the most part they have passed unregistered. It is difficult to estimate, for instance, how much of the literature of Greece was lost to us by the disappearance of the libraries of Pergamum and Alexandria. But it may be taken as certain that they represented a far wider range of material than the residuum which has been handed down by the scholars of Alexandria and Byzantium. The discoveries among papyri are already doing something, and may do more to restore what has gone. In later times, by the operation of changes of thought and the destructive agency of war, whole libraries have been destroyed entirely or exposed to the fate of books adrift in a more or less indifferent world. The Dissolution of the monasteries in England, despite the efforts of John Leland, dissipated the collections in the chief libraries of medieval England. In the sixties of the sixteenth century, Archbishop Parker and the members of the Elizabethan Society of

Antiquaries were alive to the threat to the whole of the past history of England involved in this scattering of the records, and they attempted to persuade Queen Elizabeth to found a royal library for the conservation of what remained. The attempt failed, but the petitioners went on to take this burden on their own shoulders. The Parker Library at Corpus Christi College, Cambridge, and the Cottonian Library in the British Museum were the chief contemporary results of this movement. But the activity of other scholars, inspired by the same ideals, saved the MSS. which, in the next century, flowed into the Bodleian Library at Oxford, the collections of the colleges at Oxford and Cambridge and Trinity College, Dublin, where, after strange adventures, the books of Archbishop Ussher at last came to rest, and the various private libraries which have either come intact into public collections or have again been dissipated in the sale room. The interests of these men were primarily historical or theological, and they do not seem to have made any special effort to retrieve MSS. of literary or artistic importance as such, so that much in this kind must have been lost. And, though they lived in one of the great ages of our literature, they did not anticipate the curiosity of a later time and collect manuscripts of their own day. It would never have occurred to one of these men to ask Mr. William Shakespeare of Stratford to deposit the manuscripts of the plays in his library. The survival of any written work of the writers of the Elizabethan and Jacobean periods is generally due to pure accident, or to some such circumstance as the preparation by the author himself of a calligraphically

written copy of his work for presentation to the king
or to some noble patron. It is little wonder then
that the manuscript representation of that astonishing
age is on its literary side so fragmentary.

This general loss of the script evidence of the
greatest age of our literature is to some extent com-
pensated by the fact that the printing press provided
another means to survival. For the medieval and
earlier periods this resource had not been available.
So that much has gone irretrievably. The literary
conditions of the Middle Ages were inimical to the
survival of vernacular texts. The language of culture
in those times was Latin, and MSS. in the vernacular
languages tended to suffer neglect. The main centres
of deposit were the monastic libraries, and we see
from their catalogues that their chief interest was in
Latin Books. In the earlier monastic catalogues
there is a certain proportion of vernacular literature,
and we remember with gratitude the remarkable
group of Anglo-Saxon MSS. in the catalogue of
Christ Church, Canterbury. The culture of Canterbury, however, would appear to have been rather
French than English, and in the catalogues of Christ
Church and St. Augustine's we find a remarkable
number of Anglo-Norman books entered. These
were particularly numerous at St. Augustine's. There
was one monk, Thomas Arnold, probably of the
fourteenth century, whose collection is represented
there, and it has a remarkably secular character. He
had three books of history in Latin, Guido's ' History
of the Trojan War,' the ' Chronicle of Marianus
Scotus,' and the ' Polychronicon ' of Ranulph Higden
of Chester. The rest of his gatherings were French,

and they were very nearly all romances. He had a Lancelot, a Grail romance, and Percival le Gallois, and a book of King Herlus, which may also have been Arthurian in character. Of the cycle of Charlemagne he possessed only the ' Quatre fils Aimon.' The lesser English romances were represented by the ' Ypomedon ' of Hue of Rotelande, ' Guy of Warwick ' and other tales unspecified. He had also the ' Book of William le Marshal,' that remarkable historical romance. Three other French books in his collection have no titles. Among all this plenty of romance one MS. only of Devotions in French makes a very meagre showing. Perhaps, as with another fourteenth century character, " his study was but little on the Bible." Of this interesting collection one book only has survived or at any rate has been identified, Arnold's copy of the ' Polychronicon,' which is in the University Library at Cambridge. His character for religion is saved there by the historiated initial which shows him in devotion before his patroness, St. Katherine, that woman saint whose story is itself a romance.

From these catalogues we get the impression that there was a very active French culture at Canterbury in the thirteenth and fourteenth centuries. The recovery last year of a splendid book of French poetry and prose, finely written by expert scribes in the scriptorium of Christ Church, and placed, as we shall see, in the private library of the prior of the monastery, provides us with an additional witness to the literary interests of this period. The evidence for the origin and history of this MS. depends upon a somewhat complicated argument which I will set out as succinctly as possible. This exposition may also serve as an example of the way in which slight indications may be employed to identify a manuscript which has no immediately obvious evidence of provenance with a book listed as formerly existing in a monastic library.

The great majority of the manuscripts recorded in these catalogues of the monastic libraries has disappeared, although the scholars of the sixteenth and seventeenth centuries harvested so many of them in public and private collections. There are still a number of them adrift in the world, and from time to time one of these is brought to light. In certain of these catalogues a method of identifying MSS. was adopted which still serves us to-day. All MSS. of the same text begin with the same words, but in a written, as opposed to a printed book, the second leaf will usually begin with different words. By quoting these words the librarians identified their manuscripts, and this practice has been revived by modern bibliographers. A striking instance of the use of this simple device occurred only last year. A magnificent manuscript of French poetry written in the thirteenth century was brought to the notice of the British Museum on the eve of its departure for America. It contained, among other matter, one of the best texts of Wace's 'Roman de Brut,' the Anglo-Norman rehandling of that story of Arthur which Geoffrey of Monmouth had made the most popular theme of the Middle Ages, and the longest version of the miracle play of the Resurrection, the prologue to which gives us a vivid picture of the way in which the twelfth century producer set his stage. By the generous intervention of Lord Wakefield, this MS. was saved for England. When it was examined at the Museum, it appeared to contain no obvious evidence of the place or exact date of writing. An inscription on the first page records that one Stephen Theobald of Seal near Sevenoaks gave the book, in the year 1582, to William Lambarde, the author of our first county history, the ' Perambulation of Kent.' This suggested a possibility that the MS. came from Canterbury. A study of the catalogues of the library of Christ Church, Canterbury, printed by the late M. R. James, turned this possibility into a certainty. In 1508 William Ingram, " custos martyrii " or warden of the place where St. Thomas suffered, went through the books in Archbishop Chichele's library over the Prior's Chapel at Christ Church, to pick out those that were in need of repair. From his precise description of the book-presses we can establish the fact that he found a MS., described as ' Historia Troianorum et Grecorum,' the second leaf of which began with the words " -dendum eum," on the lower shelf of the east face of the eighth press on the north side of that library. Now our book begins with a ' Hystoria Troianorum et Grecorum,' a form of Dares Phrygius, and the second leaf has these initial words. We know then that it came from Christ Church, and the exact place it occupied on the shelves of the library. But was it written there ? It cannot be identified in the early fourteenth century inventory of Prior Eastry, but in the list of the MSS. bequeathed by him to Christ Church in 1331 there appears, under the heading of " Civil Law," a ' Historia Troianorum.' This seems an odd classification for our book of romantic history until we note that the Brut is here followed by a copy of the first statute of Edward I, promulgated in the parliament which met at Westminster on April 22nd, 1275. We may be reasonably sure then that our MS. was at Christ Church before 1331 in the prior's own possession, and that it could not have been written before the early months of 1275. A search for MSS. written at Christ Church in the late thirteenth century disclosed a remarkable fact. The Cottonian MS. Galba E. iii contains a large fragment of a MS., much of the contents of which relates to that house. A chronicle of Christ Church in this MS. ends (in the original hand) in 1274, and bears evidence of having been put together in 1275. A comparison of this Cottonian MS. with the Wakefield MS. shows a very striking similarity between them. The same hands appear in both, their decoration is identical in style, the vellum on which they are written is of the same quality and is prepared to receive the writing in the same manner. The same corrector has been busy in both. They were certainly written in the same scriptorium at the same time, and it is difficult to resist the conclusion that they originally formed part of one manuscript. That manuscript was written at Christ Church in or very shortly after 1275. I have quoted this instance to show how, in a favourable case, a manuscript may come back to us after loss, with all the circumstances of its origin and the history of its transmission.

Another instance from the French literature of medieval England may be used to show the way in which the different countries of Europe at that time shared a common culture, and how the realization of

this fact may assist us in the placing of a newly recovered MS. in its proper setting. Some years ago I
was engaged upon the description of a fifteenth century
manuscript in the Irish language. One of the texts
in this MS. was the Irish version of the French
chanson de geste of Fierabras, which Whitley Stokes
had edited from this and other manuscripts of contemporary or later date. Stokes had made no
attempt to decide the immediate origin of the Irish
translation. The names of the paladins in the text
were given throughout in the Latin form, Rolandus,
Oliverus, and so forth. If the translator was using a
French text or an English version, one would hardly
expect the names to take this form. But no Latin
version of this chanson was then known to exist.
I put the question to M. Paul Meyer, who had an
unrivalled knowledge of this literature, and his answer
was that, among the few Latin versions of these
chansons known to him, there was none of Fierabras.
I then took up the rather hopeless task of attempting
to find this lost rendering. My Irish manuscripts
afforded one clue. In all the medieval copies of the
text, it was preceded by an Irish account of the
Invention of the Holy Cross. As the Fierabras
begins with an account of the bringing of relics of the
Cross to St. Denis, there seemed reason to believe
that this association was deliberate. The problem
then was to find some Latin manuscript which contained a Latin text dealing with Charlemagne and his
paladins and an account of the Invention of the Cross.
It was only after searching the catalogues of many
European libraries in vain that I turned somewhat
belatedly to the catalogue of the MSS. of Trinity

College, Dublin. There I found a brief description
of a manuscript in which were the entries :

    " De Inventione Crucis, etc."

    " Gesta Caroli Magni per Turpinum Archep. Remens."

The second text here was clearly the famous Pseudo-
Turpin, the account in Latin of Charlemagne's cam-
paign against the infidels in Spain. What did the
" etc." which followed the text of the Invention of
the Cross import ? I wrote to the librarian and asked
him to be so kind as to see if behind this " etc."
lay the Latin original of the Irish Fierabras. He
looked and found that this was indeed the case. In
the course of this investigation I had read through
the various forms which this chanson assumed in
different languages. My attention had been particularly caught by the Middle English metrical
romance, ' The Sowdone of Babylone,' a composition
of the late fourteenth century. Here there is pre-
fixed to a version of the Fierabras a rendering of
another chanson of the same cycle, the ' Destruction
of Rome,' which is found only in one manuscript,
now in the library at Hanover, where it precedes the
Fierabras. The two texts are there written in
different hands of the early fourteenth century, and
copiously illustrated with crude but vigorous drawings of a very unusual character. The manuscript
was certainly written and decorated in England. But
the English ' Sowdone of Babylone ' did not derive
from this source, for it differed in various significant
details, including the introduction of an entirely new
character. It appeared then either that the English
translator had profoundly modified his original, or
that he had used a version which has since disappeared.

At any rate I failed, as others had failed, to discover any such original, and laid the matter aside as an insoluble problem. But some years later, there came to the Museum a strange little MS. full of odd pictures which had belonged to the seventeenth century diarist, Narcissus Luttrell, and had since been in the possession of the West Country family of Pendarves. The MS. was acquired for the national collection, and I had the opportunity to examine it at my leisure and make comparisons with other forms of the texts it contained. It proved to contain the two chansons of the 'Destruction of Rome' and Fierabras, and a little examination revealed the fact that this was the intermediary between such forms as those in the Hanover MS. and the English 'Sowdone of Babylone.' The date of writing is about the middle of the fourteenth century, so that it falls neatly between the two forms of the text. And the many drawings with which it is illustrated recall in certain details the illustrations of the Hanover MS. I think you will agree that this story illustrates very well the unity of medieval culture, since an investigation which began in an attempt to find the source of an Irish text, ended in the disinterring of two unknown MSS. in Latin and French, and in the elucidation of the origins of an English poem.

It sometimes happens that a manuscript described in medieval sources and not known to be extant is found to exist still, though passing, as it were, under an alias. Perhaps the most striking example of this kind is the Codex Amiatinus of the Bible. The Venerable Bede has written for us the history of the monasteries of Wearmouth and Jarrow, his own home, which, under the rule of Benedict Biscop and Ceolfrid, had become the centre of Northumbrian culture in the seventh century. Here the Irish tradition of Iona and Lindisfarne mingled with a new stream of influence from southern Italy, whence Benedict introduced books and pictures, craftsmen and scribes. Ceolfrid was abbot in succession to Benedict from 688 to 716, and was particularly anxious to secure for his monasteries a pure text of the Vulgate, the Bible of St. Jerome. On one of his journeys he acquired a " pandect," a copy of the whole of the Scriptures. From this he had three copies made. And when in his old age, resigning his abbacy, he went upon his last journey to Rome, he took with him one of these three MSS. as a present to the Pope, no doubt as an evidence of the development of civilization in that Britain which the Roman poet, Virgil, had once described as " sundered from the whole human race." He died on the way, but his companions went on to Italy, possibly, though not certainly, to Rome, with his now posthumous gift.   These three MSS. described by Bede seemed to have completely disappeared, and the pure text of the Scriptures as introduced into England by Benedict and Ceolfrid appeared to be represented only by such MSS. as the seventh century Durham Gospels, the Book of Lindisfarne, that miracle of script and decoration, and the delightful little Gospel of St. John at Stoneyhurst which is said to have been found in St. Cuthbert's tomb in the twelfth century. Nevertheless, two of these books survived, one completely, the other in a very fragmentary form.   The Codex Amiatinus in the Laurentian Library at Florence is one of the most splendid

MSS. in the world, a huge book of 1029 leaves, measuring 19¼ by 13⅜ inches and 7 inches thick, written in two columns in a very beautiful uncial hand. An inscription of the reverse of the first leaf recorded in three elegiac couplets the presentation of the book about the year 900 by a certain Peter, abbot of a Lombard monastery, to the convent of St. Salvator of Monte Amiata. The MS. was supposed to be of Italian origin, written about the sixth century. But it was observed in modern times that the vital words which recorded the names of the monastery to which the book had been presented and of the donor, " cenobium . . . salvatoris " and " Petrus Langobardorum," not only spoilt the scansion of the verses in which they occurred, but were obviously written over erasures. The Italian scholar Bandini in 1791 suggested the reading " culmen . . . Petri," Peter's summit, a periphrasis for Rome, in the first line. But the true solution was first hit upon by de Rossi in 1886. He had been struck by the evidences of Northumbrian culture as recorded by Bede, and proposed the reading, " Ceolfridus Britonum " for " Petrus Langobardorum." Other scholars preferred " Anglorum " for "Britonum " to improve the metre, as the i of Ceolfrid is short. But the final proof was provided by Dr. Hort, who discovered in the anonymous life of Ceolfrid, which had served as the source for Bede's ' History of the Abbots,' a fuller account of the whole transaction and a copy of the verses in which the words in question read " Corpus . . . Petri," i.e. Rome as the repository of the body of St. Peter, and " Ceolfridus Anglorum," the emended form of de Rossi's reading.

The evidence was now complete, and one of the noblest MSS. of the world was vindicated for Northumbria in its great days. But what had happened to the two companion MSS. which had remained behind in Britain ? One of these seems to have disappeared for ever. But a curious discovery has restored at least some part of the other. In 1909 Canon Greenwell of Durham presented to the Museum a leaf of a fine uncial Bible which he had found in a booksellers' shop in Newcastle. Mr. W. H. Stevenson, in reporting, for the Historical MSS. Commission in 1911, upon the MSS. in Lord Middleton's possession at Wollaton Hall, called attention to eleven vellum leaves then used as bindings to volumes of estate accounts in the muniment room. These leaves were in the same hand as the Greenwell leaf, and the script and general get-up of the MS. from which they came must have been practically identical with those of the Codex Amiatinus. There can be little doubt that we have here the remains of one of the companion volumes left behind in Britain. It is pleasant to record that these Wollaton leaves were presented to the British Museum last year by the Friends of the National Libraries, and are now on exhibition in the Bible Room as an illustration of a decisive moment of the history of the Bible in these islands.

The Codex Amiatinus has been held to be the work of Italian scribes. But these fragments which are in the same script and, as their history imports, were written at the same time, must have originated in Northumbria. At most they and the Amiatinus may have been written by imported Italian scribes. But Dr. Lowe has recently shown that the uncial script here, as in various other early MSS., has certain characteristically English features. So that these manuscripts, which are among the finest of their kind, may legitimately be added to the sculptured crosses and the early poetry of Northumbria as evidence for the highly developed culture of England in the seventh and eight centuries.

This is a good instance of the way in which the survival of fragments of a lost MS. may often lead to important conclusions which have a bearing upon problems of literature and history. The binders both of MSS. in the Middle Ages and of printed books immediately after the introduction of that art were accustomed to use leaves from MSS. as flyleaves, as padding or for purposes of repair; or again the blank margins of a MS. might be used for the record of interesting matter. One of the most famous of these finds provided confirmation of a brilliant conjecture in the field of our early poetry. The Anglo-Saxon poem of ' Genesis,' a versified paraphrase of Biblical history, used to be attributed to Caedmon, the monk of Whitby, the father of English poetry. The German scholar Sievers pointed out that this could not be true, at any rate of that part of the poem known as Genesis B, which treats of the fall of the angels, for certain features of metre, grammar and syntax in this passage suggested that it derived from an original in the Old Saxon language of the Continent. Sievers supposed that there had once existed an Old Saxon paraphrase of the Old Testament, probably by the author of the New Testament paraphrase known as the Heliand. This acute conjecture was strikingly confirmed when, on the margins of a MS. in the Vatican, fragments of just this paraphrase in a hand of the ninth century were discovered, and among these fragments the actual original of a passage in the Anglo-Saxon Genesis.

Another discovery of some importance was made a few years ago in the binding of a twelfth century MS. of miscellaneous theological contents, not in itself of any remarkable interest. The flyleaves here consisted of fragments of two manuscripts, one containing parts of the Old English Martyrology in writing of the reign of King Alfred, while the other represented a MS. of much greater age and of exceptional significance. The original MS. represented by these pitiful remains must have been a magnificent codex of the letters of St. Cyprian, written in uncial letters at the end of the fourth century. A remarkable feature of this MS. was the arrangement of four columns of writing to the page, unique in Latin books, though known in such Greek MSS. as the Codex Sinaiticus. Enough of the text remained to enable its nature to be determined in a general way, and certain of the readings showed that, in three of the letters at least, the manuscript agreed with the group classified as English. It is possible that we have here all that remains of the first MS. of St. Cyprian's letters brought into England in the early days of Christianization, and becoming afterwards the basis of a particular family of the text. These three examples, which all in their different ways throw new light on the history of the early Christian culture of England, will suffice to show what results may be obtained by the careful scrutiny even of the padding of a binding.

The instances of lost and recovered manuscripts which we have been discussing hitherto are in the main of the medieval period. I have said above that with the coming of the printing press literature finds another mode of survival, and the preservation of manuscripts is no longer of primary importance. Of course much has been written since without finding a printer. So remarkable a book as Traherne's ' Centuries of Meditations ' survived only in one manuscript, and was first discovered and printed in our own day. Byron's ' Memoirs,' a book which many of us would rather see than more volumes of ' Wilhelm Meister,' was deliberately destroyed by a committee in Albemarle Street in 1824. It is not impossible that copies of it may have been made, and one of these copies may some day appear in the list of lost manuscripts recovered. Apart from such cases as these, it is not from motives of mere sentiment or a dilettante curiosity that we desire the discovery of the original manuscripts of great works of literature which have come down to us only in print. The carelessness of scribes was a constant source of corruption in texts of the manuscript period. And when the compositor displaced the scribe, he was not necessarily equipped with a more accurate habit of mind. The dramatists of the great age commonly wrote hands in which certain letters or combinations of letters were easily confused, and they spelt with a generous freedom which would have put them out of court in the simplest form of spelling bee. The compositors of that time, in their own defence, were compelled to adopt a reasonably normal spelling, and in the process of reduction from poet's spelling to printer's orthography strange things might happen to the text. The recognition of this conflict of two kinds of human nature has in our day profoundly modified the textual criticism of Shakespeare, and has increased the desire to discover the kind of hand he wrote. Attempts have been made or suggested to ferret out his manuscripts —or shall we say, having regard to the very mixed motives which have prompted some of these searches, the manuscripts of whoever wrote Shakespeare ?—in many likely and unlikely places, in violated tombs, under the beds of rivers or beneath the flags of the chancel of a country church. But no manuscript of the known plays or poems has ever appeared. Nevertheless, it has been argued by weighty authorities, and on strictly reasoned grounds, that we do possess three pages in his handwriting in a manuscript in the British Museum, the play of Sir Thomas More in the Harleian MS. 7368. If this contention can be maintained, we have recovered an invaluable aid to the textual criticism of his work, and we are relieved for ever of the wearisome assertion that anybody else but Shakespeare wrote Shakespeare. For the conditions under which these three pages were written imply that they are the original composition of a journeyman dramatist called in by his company to botch up a play to certain features of which the censor might be expected to object. And the great lawyer or the magnificent noblemen whom the wild theorists prefer to Shakespeare do not fit easily into this role.

The full discussion of all the points involved in this controversy would carry me into fields of scholarship where I have no sort of right to profess an opinion. But as one who has been under the necessity of coming to conclusions on questions of handwriting, I may perhaps be permitted to register the impression that the palaeographical arguments advanced in this controversy have made upon me.

You will remember the conditions under which this play—a very composite work as we have it—came into being. Some time about the year 1600, perhaps rather before than after that date, the dramatic company with which Shakespeare was associated proposed to produce a play dealing with certain episodes in the life of Sir Thomas More. Six different hands were employed upon this play, whether as authors, transcribers or correctors. There is some controversy as to the exact distribution of these functions, but it is clear that the original draft of the play, which is in the writing of Anthony Munday, was felt to be in danger of falling under the ban of the censor of plays, Edmund Tilney, Master of the Revels. The attempt was made to avoid this risk by extensive modifications, involving the rewriting of considerable portions of the play. The most dangerous scenes from this point of view were those dealing with the " ill-May day " anti-alien riots of 1517, and the climax of these scenes in the play as we have it now is an addition of three pages which treat of the quelling of the rioters by Sir Thomas More. It is these three pages which on various grounds are claimed for Shakespeare. The claim was first put forward in 1871 by Richard Simpson, was supported by James Spedding in 1872, and then lapsed until it was taken up again in 1916 by Sir Edward Maunde Thompson, who then, and on two later occasions, subjected the writing in these pages to a minute palaeographical scrutiny and compared them, detail by detail, with the six extant signatures of Shakespeare. In 1923 Dr. A. W. Pollard edited a book, ' Shakespeare's Hand in the Play of Sir Thomas More,' in which he himself, Dr. W. W. Greg, Sir Edward Maunde Thompson, Professors Dover Wilson and R. W. Chambers discussed the three pages from the points of view of dramatic history, palaeography, bibliography and literary criticism, and on all these points upheld the Shakespearian claim.

My concern here is with the evidence from the writing which is detailed by Maunde Thompson in a paper which is a model of minute, discreet and impartial palaeographical research. The main difficulty here, as he acknowledges, is the paucity of the material available and the particular character of that material. Shakespeare's admitted writing is known to us from six signatures alone, all of them written under rather exceptional circumstances towards the end of his life and varying from one another to an extraordinary extent. It is important to note that, in spite of this remarkable difference in the signatures, there is not the least reason for doubting that they were all written by William Shakespeare of Stratford, the author of the plays. The signatures fall naturally into two groups, the first set being attestations of legal documents, one of 1612 authenticating a deposition in a case in the Court of Requests, now in the Public Record Office, and two of 1613 on two deeds relating to the conveyance of a property in Blackfriars, now in the Guildhall and the British

Museum. The other set belongs to the year 1616, and consists of the three signatures on Shakespeare's will, now in Somerset House. The conditions under which these signatures were made are obviously not natural or ordinary. We are all nervous in the presence of lawyers, and no man writes his best on his death-bed. It has also been asserted with some show of reason that Shakespeare, in his later years, suffered from a form of writer's cramp. And he seems to have been under the delusion that, in signing his name to a deed, he ought to confine his signature to the bounds of the strip of vellum which carried the seal. All these things may account for the strange, the almost unexampled variety, in the forms and the draughts-manship of these signatures.

The problem then is to relate the script of these signatures, written by a man in his decline and under limiting circumstances, to three continuous pages claimed to have been written by the same man some ten years, at least, before in maturity and full freedom. There is something daunting to the palaeo-grapher in this statement of the conditions of the problem. No student of handwriting cares to work with signatures alone as one term of comparison. For men tend to formalize their signatures, sometimes in the direction of illegibility. And, if we want to form a true judgment of a man's script, we prefer to base our opinion on a considerable body of his writing. For the character of a man's script is determined, not by letter forms alone, but by the general flow and rhythm of his hand, the varying pressures of the pen, the spacing of his words and innumerable other details for which the narrow scope of a signature

gives no opportunity. In the case we are consider-
ing, most of these considerations cannot come into
play. We are driven back on a minute inquisition
into letter forms. In this discussion Maunde Thompson, who came to the work with an unrivalled experience of writing of all periods, is peculiarly happy.
In fact he turns the apparent weakness of the evidence,
into a source of strength, and uses the very variety
of the signatures (admitted to be the writing of one
man) as the strongest support of his case. For the
three pages are the work of a man who, as is the habit
of lively minds, did not confine himself to fixed forms,
but allowed his pen to follow the play of his mood,
changing unconsciously as his thought gathered
weight from a freer to a more deliberate style and
drawing his letters differently in different positions.
It is impossible here to go into details, and indeed
palaeographical exposition is useless without a constant reference to the originals under discussion, but
I think it may be said that a close study of Maunde
Thompson's arguments leads to the conviction that,
allowing for all the limitations of his material, he
establishes a high degree of probability that the
script of the three pages could have developed into
the writing which the six signatures, with their
curious variations, represent with the inevitable
inadequacy of their special nature and exceptional
conditions. And this perhaps is all that from the
very nature of the case could be demanded of a
palaeographer. It may be added that this probability
is strengthened into something very near to certainty
by the evidence of his collaborators. Professor Dover
Wilson shows that the misprints and odd spellings in

the good quartos of the plays, printed form Shakespeare's manuscripts, correspond to the peculiar
letter forms and letter combinations of the script of
the three pages and to their often eccentric orthography. And Professor Chambers, here and in a later
essay, contends that the movement of the thought
and the sequence of the imagery bear the evident
marks of the mind of Shakespeare and of no other
dramatist of the time. These different approaches
all converge upon the same conclusion, and I, at any
rate, feel compelled to the belief that, provisionally if
you will, pending a complete demonstration, we may
accept the contention that in these three pages we
have before us the actual writing of Shakespeare.

Here in what may be the recovered autograph of
Shakespeare we have reached the climax of Western
literature. Let us now turn back to the beginnings
and consider those discoveries of classical literature
which Hogg desired. He looked for the fulfilment of
his wishes to the buried city of Herculaneum. But
Herculaneum had already yielded all that up to our
time, at any rate, it had to give. But, if he had only
known it, the papyri which he asked his correspondent
to discover were already beginning to accumulate from
another source, the discoveries of Egyptian papyri,
which, after a false start in 1771, had already, before
he wrote his letter, yielded such treasures as the
Banksian Homer and the orations of Hyperides.

But it was not until 1891 that the full significance
of these new discoveries was revealed to the world
in general. In that year appeared the texts of
Bacchylides, the successor of Pindar, Herodas, the
contemporary of Theocritus and the sole representative

of an unknown type of Greek literature, the popular
mime, and that text on the Constitution of Athens
which revealed Aristotel in a new light as a writer
of history. From that time on the stream has never
ceased to flow, and in the past fifty years the additions to Greek literature have been greater than in
any epoch since the Renaissance, while from the
same source Biblical and early Christian studies have
received an equally remarkable enrichment. The
classical papyri must now number something like
1300, great and small, and the Biblical and early
Christian texts would bring the whole number up to
about 2000. In both fields the finds naturally vary
in importance, some being of textual interest only,
while others reveal new works or necessitate a new
approach to fundamental problems. In the first
period the emphasis of discovery was on the classics.
Five new authors were added to the canon of Greek
literature : Bacchylides, Timotheus, Hyperides, Menander and Herodas, representing the choric ode,
oratory, the New Comedy, and that other dramatic
form of the mime. And the philosopher Aristotle,
as we have seen, was shown in a new aspect. Of
known authors, Homer, Demosthenes and Euripides
are most fully represented. Of Euripides alone,
fragments of six new plays have come to light. We
have a large portion of the Ichneutae of Sophocles, a
play which reveals him in a new role as a writer of
satyric drama. Aeschylus seemed at first to have
been practically forgotten in Egypt, but recently
fragments of his work have been recovered from the
inexhaustible mounds of Oxyrhyncus. It might have
been supposed that the early lyrists writing in a

difficult dialect would have fallen out of favour, but, considerable portions of such poets as Sappho, Alcaeus and Corinna have been found among the papyri. These discoveries, and many others, have renewed and enlarged the study of Greek literature.

In recent years the outstanding discoveries in papyrology have been in the Biblical field. And of these discoveries the most remarkable, rivalling in extent and importance the great classical finds of the early period of the study, is that of the Beatty papyri. This appears to have been a chance find of a whole library of an individual or a church, and, as none of the papyri appears to be later than the mid fourth century, the collection must have been made in that century. One remarkable feature of these MSS. is that they are all codices, that is, books in the modern form of sheets of paper made up into quires, as opposed to rolls, the common form of the classical papyri. Recent investigation has indeed proved that the book was from the third century onwards the regular medium of Christian literature in Egypt. This fact had some influence on, or, at any rate, favoured the development of, the canon of the Scriptures. The roll was, for convenience sake, of an average size which did not favour the make-up of long works or collections of works in this form. A single gospel, for instance would fit easily into an ordinary roll. So that originally the books of the New Testament must have circulated as separate units. With the coming of the book a tendency to group the sacred texts is discernible. The Beatty papyri are an early example of this. They comprise remains of eleven books, three of them containing parts of the New Testament. The Testament is thus distributed among these three. The first contained the four Gospels and the Acts, the second the Pauline Epistles and the Epistles to the Hebrews, the third the Book of the Revelation. The principle of this arrangement is clear. It distributes into separate groups the historical books, those in letter form, and the single work selected to represent apocalyptic literature. The canon, as we find it in the three great codices of the fourth and fifth centuries, the Vaticanus, the Sinaiticus and the Alexandrinus, was already in process of formation. And these papyri carry back the evidence for the text of substantial portions of the New Testament to about a century before the earliest of those three codices.

Two other discoveries of papyri of small extent, but of precious content, push back the evidence for the Gospel of St. John even earlier than this. The first of these was of the two imperfect leaves and a scrap of a third leaf of another codex which has been given the name of the New Gospel. I may quote here the description of this text by Dr. H. I. Bell, its discoverer :

" These two leaves contain four different episodes. These four incidents differ markedly from each other in their relation to the canonical texts, falling in this respect into three classes. The first, a dispute between Christ and the ' rulers ' of the people, ending in an attempt to stone Him, is an incident not recorded in any of the Gospels, but the language in which it is told shows verbal parallels with St. John so close as to prove direct literary contact of one kind and another. The second and third are incidents, the healing of a leper and a question concerning the payment of dues to ' kings,' which are clearly the same as incidents related by the Synoptists, though not by St. John ; but they are related in a manner markedly different from that in the canonical Gospels. The verbal parallels which exist are mostly such as may easily be accounted for by the identity of incident, not necessarily implying that the writer borrowed from the Synoptists or vice versa ; and where, as in the third episode, we do find verbal contacts, they are with St. John, not with the Synoptists. Lastly the fourth is an incident, apparently a miracle, on the bank of Jordan, which, with one possible and very doubtful exception, shows no contacts whatever with the canonical narrative."

There has been much controversy over the exact significance of this new discovery, and its relation to the canonical Gospels cannot be said to be as yet finally established. Dr. Bell's summing up of the present state of the evidence may be quoted :

" My own conclusion, tentative, it is true, but based on a careful consideration of many points of view, is that the new text was written before the end of the first quarter of the second century ; that the author knew St. John's Gospel and possibly, but, if so, less intimately, St. Luke's or some other Synoptic Gospel ; that he had, however, access to other sources which have not survived elsewhere ; and that, though he probably handled his material quite freely, he wrote in good faith, with no heretical axe to grind."

This discovery, which has so interesting a bearing on the Gospel of St. John, was immediately supplemented by another find by Mr. C. H. Roberts in the John Rylands Library of a single leaf from a codex of that Gospel of perhaps even earlier date than the New Gospel. This not only carries back the tradition of the text, but provides evidence for the circulation of that book, written, it is generally assumed, at Ephesus towards the end of the first century, among Egyptian Christians within fifty years of its composition.

The general effect of these discoveries is that we have been brought a century and more nearer to the original writing down of the New Testament Scriptures, have acquired new and valuable material for textual criticism, and have been given a new insight into the process of formation of the canon of the Bible.

This lecture has, I am afraid, been somewhat discontinuous, but I may perhaps claim that the nature of the subject makes this unavoidable. For lost manuscripts come to light suddenly and unexpectedly and with no nice observation of order. The instances I have given have been drawn in the main from the experience of the last fifty years, and they could have been increased in number, had time permitted. The conclusion seems to be that we live in a remarkable age of discovery in many fields, and that there is every reason to believe that finds of an equal importance to those with which I have dealt still lie before us. A clever girl like Mary Meredith, *née* Peacock, would find plenty to exercise her wits upon if she applied herself to any branch of manuscript studies to-day.

THE TREDEGAR MEMORIAL LECTURE FOR 1939.

The Tredegar Lecture perpetuates the honoured memory of the first Viscount Tredegar of the second creation. It was founded in 1935 by his son, the second Viscount, a Fellow of this Society since 1928.

THE DIGNITY OF ENGLISH THOUGHT.

BY MICHAEL ROBERTS.

[Read January 24th, 1940.]

"To guard the purity of the English tongue and the dignity of English thought." To guard them from whom or from what? When, in 1924, the Marquess of Crewe used these words to describe the aims of the Royal Society of Literature he did not explain them, nor did he ask whether the purity of the English tongue should be safeguarded at the expense of its flexibility and accuracy, or whether the dignity of English thought was more important than its clarity, percipience and truthfulness. At a casual reading it might seem that the aims of the Society, as Lord Crewe expressed them, were negative and restrictive rather than positive and expansive, the aims of old age rather than those of maturity or youth, the aims of the pedant rather than the philosopher, the academic critic rather than the poet.

It would be rash to assume that such aims are wrong, or that a society having these aims would necessarily be the enemy of all new and truthful writing. In literature, as in a democratic constitution, there is a need for a system of checks and balances : innovations must be questioned ; the lessons of history and tradition must be reiterated ; and our speech must be preserved from the distortions of narrow kinds of accuracy and from the obscurity and clumsiness of elaborate precision. The poet, like any other enthusiast, must be kept under strict surveillance, for his use of words is intended to express his own peculiar vision, and he does not always consider the effect of his peculiar usages on language in general.

The King's English, like the King's Highway, must serve the common need, and the common man must have his watchdogs. And whereas the poet is, from the nature of his work, an anarchist and an individualist, the literary police who guard the English language from the violence of his innovations fall naturally into organizations, academies and Royal Societies. They are conservative, and having no personal vision to express, they help to preserve the general standard of education and literacy ; but at the same time exert a repressive influence on art and literature, and among contemporary writers they are inclined to honour those who imitate the discoveries of the past rather than those who make discoveries of their own. If we conceive of dignity as nothing more than marmoreal insensibility, it is plain that a society which exists to preserve the dignity of thought will do its best to oppose all thought whatever, and nothing but its own insensibility will prevent it from succeeding ; it will be dullness incarnate.

To interpret the aims of the Society in this narrow

sense, however, is neither kind nor useful. " Purity " is a curious and fascinating word, and its emotive power has given force to some queer heresies ; but the word " dignity " is at least of equal interest and has had far less attention. If we examine the conception of " dignity " with some care we may find, as we instinctively feel, that Lord Crewe's statement was something more than a rhetorical plea for ponderous inactivity. The dictionary cannot help us, for " dignity " is one of those words that exist in their own right and are coloured by a wealth of association and implication that can only be revealed through innumerable quotations. It is embedded in the English language, and cannot be torn out and replaced by some other group of words. Honesty, age, courage, prosperity and popular respect, all these enter into the notion of civic dignity, but no combination of these qualities itself constitutes the dignity of a citizen ; and in the same way the dignity of thought is something different from clarity, acumen and truthfulness, something more than self-consistency and comprehensiveness, and of no less value.

In our special problem there are two main aspects of dignity to consider ; there is the public dignity of thought, the respect and esteem in which thought itself is held, and there is the intrinsic quality on which that popular esteem is, or should be, based. The public dignity of thought is not so much a characteristic of thought itself as of society. It is measured not merely by the degree of popular esteem, but by the quality and percipience of that esteem. Sometimes we are tempted to sacrifice the percipience and accuracy of thought rather than run the risk of alienating people who prefer statements that are familiar, comforting and simple, to others that are strange, disturbing and complex. But dignity purchased in this way is worthless ; popular esteem is of no value unless it rests on the recognition of intrinsic dignity ; and dignity in this sense implies proportion and balance as well as all the familiar qualities of reputable thinking.

In this it resembles the integrity of a self-respecting citizen. It is not alien to other intrinsically valuable qualities, indeed it cannot exist without them, but is something more than the sum of these qualities. It implies a just proportion between these qualities ; and more than that, it implies a capacity for meeting circumstances without abandoning or amending one's fundamental attitude to life. The dignity appropriate to the soldier or the captain of a sinking ship presupposes ordinary courage, competence and devotion ; but it is distinct from all these. It is something superadded, a gesture of excess—the Captain of the *Courageous* lifting his arm to salute the flag as his ship goes down ; Nelson refusing to hide his decorations. In every instance there is something at first sight unnecessary and almost stupid—a refusal, beyond a certain point, to struggle to preserve one's own life. Nelson might have removed his medals as the British fighting forces are ordered to do to-day. What was the value of his gesture ? What has it in common with the dignity of a statesman who refuses to meet an unfair argument with a smart retort, or with the dignity of an ordinary man who refuses to run for a train ?

Fundamentally, all these are gestures of confidence ; they show that the will of a man is not wholly at the mercy of physical and moral infirmity and the accidents of an indifferent universe. There is a price to be paid for escaping death in battle or postponing it in the Antarctic ; there is a price to be paid for crushing a political opponent or catching a train ; and sometimes the price is too high. Dignity in this sense is an assertion that there are some things more valuable and more durable than our own lives and our own convenience. It is not a matter of intelligent and resolute devotion to some professed purpose. No doubt Nelson's action helped to invigorate the English nation and the English Navy for more than a century, but we can hardly say that that was Nelson's aim, and the dignity of his action is as clear and inspiring to a German or a Frenchman as to an Englishman. It was an assertion that life and relative safety were not worth having at the price of subterfuge and an unsailorly disordering of habit. In the same way, the man who refuses to run for a train preserves a just proportion between his immediate purpose and his conception of the conduct becoming to a man of his particular quality.

Dignity thus depends on maintaining a sense of proportion without submitting to circumstance ; and the conduct that we call dignified depends on the general framework of ideas and the purposes that most closely touch the man concerned. In accepting a risk willingly (or even flamboyantly) not strictly necessary to his duties, Nelson demonstrated human dignity in general ; but he also showed the specific dignity of a sailor. The line between cowardice and judicious caution is not easily drawn, and to Nelson, as a fighting sailor, it was important not to draw it to his own advantage. One might almost say that a certain narrowness is characteristic of dignity, not the narrowness of ignorance but that of abnegation. The Admiral refuses to use methods that are in general inappropriate to his calling, even though they might for a moment suit his purpose. The statesman refuses to use the methods of the cheap-jack and the low comedian.

This rigid observance of a code is easily mistaken for stupidity, and indeed it does become stupidity if the code is not of greater value than the life or comfort of the individual. The modes in which qualities like intelligence, mercy and courage manifest themselves must depend on circumstance, and there is no virtue in the pigheaded performance of an unmoded line of conduct. Don Quixote has dignity because he was standing for virtues that were being lost in the new age ; but he also maintained some superficial manners that did not really represent those virtues. His dignity was the specific dignity of a Christian knight, and in the age of Cervantes the conception of Christian knighthood was already being replaced by that of the Christian gentleman, or that of the gentleman *tout court*. His hero was dignified in making no fundamental concessions to changing circumstances : he was silly in not recognizing any change at all. To be in too great a hurry to amend one's manners shows a lack of confidence in the principles that underlie those manners ; never to change at all is merely stupid, and shows no understanding of the obligations of good conduct and good thought.

Dignity is shown not merely by some such gesture of confidence, but by a gesture within a given mode : a traditional and honourable form of conduct is maintained in circumstances that are strange and almost incongruous. In the same way, although the inner dignity of thought depends partly on scope, consistency and accuracy, and partly on balance and proportion, it is shown through self-reliance. There are times when the methods of reason fail in our hands, and we are justified in appealing to prejudice or self-interest or coercion, but if we appeal to these we are ourselves denying the arbitrament of reason. If we do so in the name of reason, and not of our own personal convenience, we are betraying the dignity of thought. We are revealing either that we no longer believe that reason and justice can rely upon their own authority, or that we have no confidence in the reason and justice of our own case.

Dignity is thus related to authority : to throw away one's dignity, whether it be the dignity of a soldier, a mathematician or a churchman, is to risk losing one's proper authority ; to call in an alien kind of authority, as when the diplomat calls in the soldier, the churchman calls in the policeman, and the philosopher calls in the advertising expert or the social snob, is to admit that the original authority is not able to deal with the problems in the field to which it lays claim. The bigger our original claims, the greater our loss of dignity when we abandon our proper kind of authority. The poet or scholar who brings a libel action against a bad reviewer is more undignified than the hack novelist who takes a similar course. Furthermore, our loss of dignity increases the farther we move from our original authority. The poet and the scholar claim that the ultimate power of persuasion is found in their own use of words ; if they resort to sarcasm, scurrility or facetiousness they are making a tacit admission that the authority of their own particular kind of writing has its limits ; if they call in the help of the law, they are admitting the limitation of all discussion, whether reasoned or emotional ; if they horsewhip their opponent, they are abandoning the claims of law as well as literature, and losing the distinction between their own authority and that of the prize-fighter and the assassin.

To call in an alien authority deliberately and consciously is a gesture of no-confidence, an admission that events have passed beyond the control of our own specific methods ; and even when the appeal is made unconsciously and the false authority is not seen to be alien, the gesture is undignified and acts to the detriment of the true authority. The temptation to rely on false authority is always strong, for we are none of us purely poets or philosophers or mathematicians ; other interests sometimes creep in and warp our judgment, and weapons which are not those of thought are always at hand. If we oppose some argument or doctrine, we are apt to meet it on the lowest instead of the highest level ; even if we put aside our obvious self-interest, we do not like to consider facts and arguments that will make some of our own work useless, and we are tempted to use our seniority and social dignity to belittle younger men. Similarly, if we are young ourselves, we are tempted to assert the importance of our own generation, and to betray the dignity and competence of our own thought by ignoring facts and problems that give weight and authority to the older generation. Writers, critics and philosophers are advocates before a jury only too willing to be influenced by false rhetoric and irrelevant prejudice, and there is no judge to puncture pomposity and restore the airy nothings to their due proportion.

In the world in which philosophy and literature struggle for their existence the use of false authority is a commonplace, and our own educational system does little to counteract it. Big sales are deliberately confused with merit, until we have a generation which honestly does not know of any other standard. Unless we encourage people to make use of the judgments of others better qualified than themselves and to discriminate among authorities, we cannot expect them to judge a poet by anything but his eccentricities, or a mathematician by anything but the length of his beard, the number of his degrees, and the extent of his absent-mindedness. In any ordered hierarchy the higher authorities have a responsibility to the lower, just as the lower themselves have the responsibility for discrimination. The business of the able mathematician is not merely to produce good mathematics, but also to see that the " lower orders " are not deceived by charlatans and do not confuse mathematics and theosophy, or astronomy and astrology. But to-day ordinary people are seldom taught to discriminate among authorities ; their newspapers teach them not to discriminate, and learned societies seldom think it their duty to contradict the downright lies and deliberate confusion of authorities that are found in publishers' blurbs

and in advertisements beginning " Science teaches
us . . . ."

To maintain the public dignity of thought implies a
resumption of the responsibility of leadership ; but
the problem of maintaining the internal dignity of
thought is no less pressing. It is not enough to pursue
our own particular study to the best of our ability :
the *proportions* of thought need to be maintained,
independently of political and economic pressure, for
culture implies something more than an energetic
refinement of thought and observation—an industrious
stamp-collector or a brilliant chemist is not necessarily cultured—and something more than a wide-
spread recognition of specialized authorities. A man
is not said to be cultured unless he has a variety of
activities and perceptions and has kept a sense of the
relative proportions of those activities ; and a nation's
culture cannot be said to be healthy unless it shows a
similar wealth and proportion.

But the dignity of *English* thought ? In what
sense does English thought differ from European
thought, and ought we to maintain the differences ?
No doubt there are times when the dignity of English
thought is best maintained by learning as quickly as
possible all that the rest of Europe can teach us.
There is no dignity in the narrow-minded ignorance
and the weakness for home-made religion and philosophy that have often been characteristic of these
islands. But in its traditional distrust of verbal
ingenuity, its emphasis on charity and the civic
virtues, its willingness to submit to fact, and its
insistence on the ultimate value of works as well as
faith, English thought has always differed a little

from that of France or Italy or Germany. The tradition of Duns Scotus, Ockham and Roger Bacon, the tradition of Shakespeare, Johnson and Coleridge, differs from that of Aquinas, Dante and Machiavelli as an oak-tree differs from a cedar.

Here, too, the dignity of our thought needs to be maintained by active effort ; under the influence of industrialism the tree has grown misshapen—one side has developed out of all proportion to the other. We have gained in our understanding of inanimate nature ; we have gained in the physical sciences and perhaps in sympathetic understanding of our neighbours, but our interest in poetry and religion has withered, and our knowledge of ourselves has been obscured by brilliant parasitic growths. It is not that we have borrowed from Rousseau or Hegel, Galileo, Marx or Freud, but rather that we have failed to assimilate our borrowings and impregnate them with our own traditional wisdom. The English writers we have mentioned, including Johnson, were all great borrowers, but they incorporated their borrowings into the English tradition. To-day it is doubtful whether we can really talk of an English tradition at all, for we have divided into factions, schools and parties, just as our society has divided into divergent groups and classes ; and those divergences, which spring from narrow-minded specialization and a lack of general responsibility, tend to perpetuate their causes.

In whatever sense we interpret the word " dignity," we see that the dignity of English thought is to-day in serious danger, and if we wish to restore it our task is complex. We have to maintain the autonomy of thought by resisting every temptation to gain a point

by an appeal to wit or prejudice, social or financial
prestige, legal or illegal force ; we have to maintain
or build up a popular respect for thought based on
the recognition of specific authorities, and we have
to restore a just proportion between the different
fields of knowledge.

These tasks are particularly difficult in our own
time. The last twenty or thirty years have seen the
intrusion of new ideas in philosophy, in politics, in
art, and those ideas have influenced all classes of
society. Tradition has been challenged and asked
to produce its credentials ; religion has come to be
regarded as a toy for old ladies and young children ;
scientific methods and pseudo-scientific methods have
been applied in fields that were once the preserve of
literary judgment. Newtonian physics has given
place to something at once more comprehensive and
less comprehensible ; introspective psychology has
taught us to doubt our deepest impulses, and to see
doubtful or disreputable motives behind apparent
altruism ; and the study of economics has introduced
into politics something of the ungainly and disruptive self-consciousness that psychology has brought
into private morality.

All these changes have seemed to be something
more than isolated innovations ; they have appeared
to be part of an immense and ramifying assault on a
whole order of thought and society ; and at the same
time, the unity of thought has failed. Not merely
have the specialized studies passed beyond the range
of vision of the cultured amateur (that would not,
in itself, be serious), but they have fortified or given
rise to attitudes and outlooks incompatible with each

other and based on widely divergent conceptions of reality and value. Perhaps the most characteristic outlook of our time is that in which the absolute has been replaced by the relative. To see that our own judgments are valid only in relation to our own particular problem is a necessary part of the pursuit of generality, but " virtue " and " beauty " have shared the fate of " scientific truth," until, by a curious combination of emotional and logical *non sequiturs*, people have come to feel that nothing is good or true or beautiful except for a purpose that can be defined ; and since they cannot define an ultimate purpose they begin to feel that nothing is good or true or beautiful at all.

This so-called " disillusion," in the midst of intense and confusing activity in all the diverse fields of art and thought, has combined with social causes to reduce popular respect for scholarship and aesthetic sensibility ; and the classes most deeply influenced have been those on whom the arts and sciences once rested. The circulation figures for any great library or any serious literary periodical show that between 1918 and 1939 the " serious reading public " declined to something like a third of its original size. In part, this decline in the authority of thought has been a consequence of the activity of thought itself ; and one reply to it has been a return to instinct and intuition and a revulsion of feeling against doctrines once put forward as emancipated and enlightened. For those who defend the autonomy of thought the reply cannot be so simple ; but we must be prepared to admit that some beliefs and aims that we believed to be wholly good, both in themselves and in their consequences, may be based on fallacies and on false or inadequate premises.

The prospect of engaging in a real defence of the dignity of thought is not pleasant ; it involves the recognition of a deeply-rooted social malady ; but the alternative is to assume that the decline follows from causes wholly beyond our control, and to make such an assumption is to abandon all claims that we have ever made on behalf of poetry and knowledge. We cannot take a fatalistic view of the decline of our culture without demonstrating, however unwittingly or unwillingly, that our culture is in fact anaemic and unworthy of respect, nor can we effectively defend the dignity of thought by any but the weapons of thought itself.

If, while preserving the inner dignity of thought, we are to re-establish its outer dignity, we must look for ideas to combat, not men to imprison ; and those ideas will be false ideas that infect our own thought, or true ideas pushed beyond their proper field or emphasized out of due proportion.   We cannot expect to find that the causes of decline are in ideas foreign to our own minds, for the popular thought of an age is a by-product of the most serious and best-informed thought of previous ages.   It is our own heritage that is at fault, for a system of thought that allows itself to degenerate into falsehood when popularized is itself unsatisfactory.

Here we meet our real difficulty : in the past century " popular thought " has become more and more important, until it has seriously undermined the authority of good art and good scholarship. True, all that we have done in the past hundred years has not yet established a democracy, but has merely broadened the basis of oligarchy. But the broadening has gone far beyond the original limit of that upper-class society which was the ground-layer or foundation of literary and scientific authority in the eighteenth century ; and while we have been extending the *political* foundations of society, we have done very little towards integrating the additions into the cultural scheme. At a time when the economic and political power of the lower-middle class is strong enough to influence the direction of national effort, the basis of educated upper-class responsible opinion, on which the authority of the arts and sciences once rested, is no longer a sufficient support for a national culture ; but even to-day the higher authorities— including the Royal Society of Literature—do not always realize their own responsibilities in face of the illiteracy and irresponsibility of the Press.

In so far as we have achieved democracy at all, it is a pluto-democracy ; and in a pluto-democracy all the specific authorities tend to become consolidated into one, the authority of wealth. Pluto-democracy may be the social order that gives the freest and most effective expression to the wishes of the majority ; but even at its best it leads to a confusion of authorities ; the authority that a man earns as a manufacturer of ice-cream or motor-cars is convertible at will into authority in the fields of statesmanship or learning. He can endow professorships and laboratories and so encourage one kind of study at the expense of others ; he can turn the mind of a nation away from poetry into chemistry, or out of chemistry into religion. He cannot always dictate the answers, but he can dictate the questions that engage a nation's attention ; and in spite of occasional and honourable attempts by men like Nobel to undermine the source of their own wealth, he is likely to encourage the kind of study on which his own money-making was based.

Again, the pluto-democratic faith encourages the belief that all desires are free and equal, that my opinion is as good as yours, and that " authority," in the sense in which we are using the word, does not exist ; but it goes further and destroys the sense of moral responsibility. We do not accept the crude argument that whatever pays is right, but we do accept the more insidious argument that " a man must live," and we allow glib talk about " economic pressure " and " the tendency of the time " to excuse the deliberate encouragement of pettiness, sentimentality and false reasoning. The dignity of thought cannot exist without the sense of authority, and the sense of authority cannot exist without the sense of responsibility ; but the popular newspapers of this country have done their best to destroy that sense. " News " is no longer the accurate information a citizen needs in order to realize and fufil his responsibilities ; it is anything that amuses him or excites strong emotions, or enables him to ignore his own responsibility by blaming other people.

There is no need to call in any moral code to condemn this exploitation of frivolity, laziness and vanity ; even if we admit no ultimate good except human survival, time has its own defences. There is the force of experience—some beliefs that readily commend themselves to the simple mind are plainly false and frustrate the aim that they are meant to

serve ; and there is the force of tradition, which is the
accumulated wisdom of our ancestors. These two
defences are not different in kind ; the authority of
the chemist or the engineer is demonstrated by the
fact that his predictions are fulfilled, whereas those
of the crank are not ; the authority of the philosopher
and the prophet, though it seems to rest on nothing
more than tradition, is in the long run demonstrated
by experience. The wanton disregard of tradition
is as damaging to the dignity of thought as the wanton
disregard of familiar fact ; and the damage will
produce results that everyone will recognize as bad,
whether they value the dignity of thought or not.
Whatever the changes in our social structure may be,
experience will compel us in the end to recognize
the value of tradition ; we cannot repeat in every
generation all the experiments and errors of our
fathers, nor can we expect to remember for ever all
the proofs and all the evidence ; we must take something for granted if we are to add a little to the
traditional wisdom. Carried beyond a certain point,
scepticism and the spirit of liberal inquiry demonstrate
nothing but the inability of the human race to learn
from experience.

To reflect that time will correct our faults and
follies is, however, neither a consolation nor an
excuse for inaction. An evil is always irreparable ;
and we need to admit that the spirit of free inquiry,
though it has led to immense discoveries, has often
helped to destroy the sense of value by undermining
the traditional prestige of activities that call for
initial discipline and arduous training. For this the
responsibility rests not only on those who deliberately

exploit human weaknesses for the sake of a quick profit, but also on those who, though devoted to the dignity of thought, nevertheless betray it through a short-sighted acquiescence in the fashionable beliefs of the day. In our age, in which a man can make a fortune in a few years and leave others to pay for the consequences, long-sightedness is not a popular virtue ; and the resulting disregard of traditional wisdom and traditional values is reinforced by the prestige of laboratory sciences whose findings can be tested at will.

Democracy, even in the form of pluto-democracy, has at least one great merit ; it cannot long continue without placing heavy responsibility on the individual. Unless the democratic faith is based on respect for the specific authorities of religion, the sciences and the arts, unless it rests on something more solid than pragmatism, subjectivism and hedonism, and unless the ordinary man is taught to realize his responsibilities, it must lead to social and intellectual disintegration. " Things fall apart, the centre cannot hold," said Yeats in one of his later poems, and if we were not in the habit of belittling all the poets and philosophers of our own age, we might have listened earlier.

Instinctively men feel the dangers of such a situation before they see it clearly, and the instinctive reaction is not always wise. In Germany and Italy there have been revolutions claiming to restore authority and faith ; but they have restored one authority, not many, and the faith is faith in national aggrandisement. In America, France and England there is still time to avoid the mistakes of others and profit

by their experiments.   In these countries the disintegration is more manifest in the field of art and thought
than in the world of politics and industry, and we
can deal with it if we recognize its causes.

The decline in public respect for all forms of critical
and philosophic thought is only one example of the
immense and complicated changes in European society
in the past 150 years.   Literary culture has ceased to
be a prerogative of the upper class ; it has not yet
become a national possession—an English factory-
hand does not boast of Shakespeare and Locke as the
corresponding Frenchman would boast of Descartes
and Racine.   Our social structure is changing, and
the old upper class no longer feels a proprietary right
in the literature and science of its own day ; it looks
towards the past rather than the future, and in its
anxiety to retain political and financial power it
refuses the responsibilities of intellectual leadership.
In the special sciences little harm is done, for these
are already firmly based on a hierarchy that reaches
down to the masses of the people ; and in this field
the only threat comes from the general coarsening of
thought.   But in the imaginative arts the position is
different, and one sign of the abdication of the upper
class is the increasing tendency to evade the responsibility of judgment by saying that we must wait for
the verdict of posterity.   But the mere passage of
time does not sift out the good books from the bad,
and if the good books are lost now, through lack of
readers or lack of a publisher, they will never come
into existence at all, and their absence will be reflected
in an increasing crudity in our national thought.

Meanwhile the newly educated classes are still

incapable of taking over the intellectual functions of a governing class. The only dignity they are taught to appreciate and emulate is social and financial ; in art and thought they ape their financial betters. That which was accepted and valued by the upper classes thirty years ago, the newly-educated classes accept and value to-day. In England the appreciation and understanding of the specific dignities of the liberal arts is not yet part of our elementary and secondary education. In France, partly because the French democratic tradition is in some ways older than ours, the position is a little better ; the schools are the foundation of a pyramid of intellectual authority, and one reason why academies are more active in France than here is that they come under sharper and better-informed public scrutiny.

Secondary education in England is barely forty years old, and the burden thrown on it by the intellectual abdication of the upper class has been increased by the fact that parents more and more leave the *whole* education of their children to the schools. We have many thousands of devoted teachers, but not all of them are cultured in the older sense of the word, and most of them feel that it is their duty to produce successful wage-earners rather than responsible citizens. The public boarding-schools have often been attacked for producing a " type," but it was a type that not only served a social purpose but also had a sense of social and intellectual responsibility. The secondary schools, on the other hand, are merely helping poorer boys to " get on "—they must get matriculation, they must win scholarships, anything to escape from the class from which they come. There

is very little place for " the dignity of thought " in
such a system, and how many of us are doing anything
to maintain it or restore it ?

Here and there we find exceptions—the good schoolmaster, conscious of the problems of his own time,
the good pupil who finds his way unguided to the
authors whose works are a record of the intelligence,
sensibility and charity of past generations.   But what
are we doing to build up a competent, critical public
to replace the dwindling upper-class public ?   To what
extent are we ourselves aware of the changes that are
undermining a cultural system based on hereditary
aristocracy ?   To what extent are the ideas of
democracy themselves false and stultifying ?   From
Walter Bagehot and Matthew Arnold down to T. S.
Eliot and R. G. Collingwood we have had authors
who could see the problems and state them clearly,
but have we taken these authors seriously ?   True,
the works of men like Matthew Arnold are " set
books " for school examinations ;   but is anyone
taught to feel that the problems with which Arnold
deals are real problems, and that his answers have a
real authority ?   Do the teachers themselves feel it ?
Is it not true to say that teachers and pupils alike
feel that the ultimate responsibility for discrimination
and action rests on someone else, and that as far as
they are concerned the dignity of thought can be
left to take care of itself?

To-day it is no longer possible to believe that everything is automatically getting better.   The scientific
discoveries of the nineteenth century gave us a large
dose of freedom—free trade, free speech, free thought.
The advance of science and the expansion of industry

depended on a spirit of free inquiry and almost unrestricted economic freedom for the manufacturer. But this " freedom " has been extended far beyond the field in which it was appropriate. It is necessary now to recognize the natural limits of freedom. Thought, for example, is never really free : it may turn in one direction or another to suit the needs of the moment, but it is governed by irreducible facts. A man can hold a silly belief all his life and to all appearances be none the worse for it, but a nation of half-baked free-thinkers, astrologers, flat-earthers, will ultimately suffer materially as well as intellectually. It may be true that the untutored mind " knows the highest," but as T. E. Hulme pointed out, unless the ordinary man is egged on by tradition and discipline he does precious little about it. Hulme regarded this need for authority as an aspect of the Christian doctrine of original sin. In different ways we find the same view of human nature emphasized in Hobbes and Pascal, Pope and Johnson. But the dominant view to-day is very different. Man is regarded as naturally good, and driven to evil courses only by poverty and lack of education. Even his accidental shortcomings are glossed over : the crude democratic or plutocratic faith asserts that what the ordinary man wants is right, and that the problem of government is merely one of ascertaining those wants and satisfying them. Such, in principle, is the basis of liberalism and communism, and in practice the basis of conservatism too. Whether that basis is false is a problem for thought, but when we begin to think about it our vanity intervenes : it may well be that Pascal and Johnson are right, and that responsibilities are as important as privileges and as necessary to a satisfying life, but the school of Montaigne and Rousseau which values self-expression above self-control is more flattering. The "progressive" reader labels the disquieting and classical Mr. Eliot "reactionary," and turns back to the more comfortable romantic view that finds its various expressions in Shelley, Marx and H. G. Wells.

But is the romantic view tenable ? Can man be made the measure of the universe, without any absolute standards by which he and his purposes can be judged ? Or must we, in the last resort, admit a need for dogma and tradition ? This has been the major problem of English criticism in the past twenty-five years ; and from 1925 to 1935 it was debated on a high level of dignity and sincere inquiry, in *The Criterion*, *The Adelphi*, *The Calendar of Modern Letters*, *The Hound and Horn*, and *Symposium*. One by one these periodicals have ceased publication or disappeared from the bookstalls : there is no paper in England to-day in which such a discussion could be conducted without recourse to frivolity, petty spite and irrelevant snobbery. But the debate, though it attracted little attention from the academic and social world, was not useless. The contributions of Paul Elmer More, T. S. Eliot, I. A. Richards and John Middleton Murry were not merely debating speeches, designed to make the other man look a fool ; they were sincere attempts to discover the truth, or those aspects of the truth most relevant to our time ; and although the dispute was not new, and may never be finally resolved, it did in this instance end in something like general agreement. The romantic and

Utopian view may still be the popular view among our older newspaper critics and our older politicians; but among those willing to listen to argument the anti-romantic view has prevailed.

Whether the popular respect for thought is still deep enough to enable that view to become effective in a reasonable time, one cannot say. The disease of our society is deep and complex, and Matthew Arnold's failure is enough to remind us how little the views of a few poets and literary critics can influence a nation. But Arnold was working against a nation apparently prosperous in its philistinism, a nation in which the cracks in society were barely perceptible. To-day the political confusion of our society is obvious; the romantic ideas of humanism have ended in weariness and disillusion; the inability of a nation to live without a core of positive belief resting on something more than self-interest is reflected in a growing feeling that life is not worth while, and this in turn finds expression in a falling birth-rate.

It is possible to view all this pessimistically; to believe that it is too late to make any change, to believe that this loss of confidence, responsibility and the sense of authority is irrevocable and that the forces of pluto-democracy will stifle the voice of reason before it can be heard. But it is equally possible to say that the time is ripe for a change of outlook as profound as that which happened at the Renaissance. The human being is stupid, but he also has common sense; he may forget the wisdom of his ancestors, but he will learn it again from experience. The social order is crumbling; but not before a new social order is coming into being. Authority of every kind has decayed, but only because we have been living in a period of transition from a purely agricultural to a partly industrial society. There is no reason to expect the *tempo* of scientific invention to be maintained. Some of the limits of profitable mechanical invention have almost been reached, and already there is reason to believe that the best brains of the younger generation are turning, not towards physical sciences, but to economics, philosophy and history. If, as seems likely, the world of the future is more stable than that of the past century, there will be time for populations to become stabilized, to produce a culture in key with their environment, and to modify their environment to suit their personal needs. There will be time to think and recognize the dignity of thought.

If all this happens, our conception of culture will necessarily change : the value that we place on physical science will perhaps decline, whereas our valuation of the disinterested vision of the artist and the long-sighted vision of the prophet will perhaps be higher. There will be less demand for a world of sugary make-belief, for there will be a little less external ugliness to ignore. There will be more demand for vicarious excitement to make up for the lost thrills of desperate competition. The fields of poetry and humour will change a little, and some reputations will be diminished and some enhanced. But it cannot be said that the dignity of thought will necessarily suffer.

To maintain that dignity in the midst of great historical changes is a worthy activity, but it cannot be done by passive resistance to new ideas, nor can it be done by the acute exercise of the disinterested intelligence alone. The exercise of active thought is always something more than an intellectual game : it involves changes of feeling, alterations in the direction and depth of our insight, a revision of moral acumen, and a redirection of energy. To think a new thought is easy ; to reorientate our life and accept a new responsibility is hard and unwelcome : it is a sacrifice of our familiar self, and we postpone it as we might postpone an operation that would leave us healthier but weaker. For that reason we need not only critical thought, but also poetry ; and the poetry that represents the acceptance of a new outlook will always be revolutionary. It cannot be merely a reversal of old statements within the old forms ; the kind and quality of the sentiments must change, the dominant imagery must be different, the rhythms must be consonant with a new mode of action ; and for the moment the differences that mark it off from the poetry of the immediate past may be big enough to make it seem not to be poetry at all to those who are deeply committed to an older view.

There is no doubt that poetry of this kind has been written in our own time, but the influence of poetry is very small in an age in which the mechanical sciences have scored such quick and spectacular successes. Some of the new poetry of our age is unpopular not merely because it *is* poetry, nor because it is difficult to understand, but because it represents a real change of feeling and valuation, which people are reluctant to make. They cannot even see what is asked of them, and they fail to understand that the poetry of T. S. Eliot and the later poetry of Yeats is not an attack on " beauty," but the necessary complement of an intellectual outlook that differs radically from that of Shelley, G. B. Shaw or H. G. Wells.

Perhaps we are all inclined to exaggerate the differences between the poetry of our own age and that of the past ; to those in the struggle, every war is the Great War. Under the eye of history it may seem that we have moved by barely imperceptible steps, whereas to ourselves we seem to have been jolted out of one planetary system into another. One function of thought and of an academic group within society is to achieve detachment from the excitements and exaggerations of the day ; the " dignity of thought " must rise superior to the catastrophes of politics. But to preserve a detached historical judgment, or to reveal society to itself with the unbiased vision of the poet or the artist, is not the same thing as remaining indifferent to right and wrong, truth and falsehood, in the world about us. In our age, in which the dignity of thought is seriously threatened both within ourselves and in the world outside, it is specially necessary to be sure that our thinking is an act of the whole man, not a superficial readjustment of verbal tokens. If we find ourselves in intellectual opposition to the prevailing outlook of this age, we need the language and the living imagery of those poets who have taken up the same position as ourselves. As a general needs to see the landscape like a map, so we need to see our own problems and our own actions under the eye of history; but we need also the passionate apprehension of poetry ; without it, the dignity of thought becomes sterile, brief and brittle, like a monument of rubble.

Conversely, though it is not our business as poets, critics and philosophers to concern ourselves with practical problems of politics and economics, we need to understand something of those problems ; it is not our business to join in the reiteration of slogans, but we need to see our own problems within the historical framework, and to ask what adjustment of attitude and effort a body like the Royal Society of Literature must make if it is to preserve the values for which it stands. We have to admit—as this Society often has admitted—that up to the present we have failed, and we have to set to work to build up on a new and wider foundation the authority of literature and the proper proportions of national thought. We need to controvert the popular superstition that the natural thoughts and feelings of the unreflecting man are always right and good ; we need to controvert also the belief that a simulacrum of the good literature of the past is itself good literature ; and we must get rid of the fatal and fatalistic superstition that posterity will do our work for us.

The collapse of one system of ideas, the failure of the egalitarian, hedonistic and romantic outlooks, the simultaneous change in the order of society, does not mean that all we value is lost ; it merely means that some of our calculations were based on inadequate knowledge, and that some were considered finished when they were scarcely started. In thought, a position of dignity must be one that calls for no sudden and ignominious reversal in face of changing circumstances ; and for that reason it must rest on moral, aesthetic and scholarly authority and on the wisdom of tradition. If indeed the day were over when thought could wield its own authority, and if the future could promise nothing except narrowness and irresponsibility, the public confusion of all forms of authority into one, and the exercise of misshapen ingenuity like the monstrous growth of a diseased plant, it would still be worth while to resist the current of our time. Thought, in the sense of an acute and responsible understanding of the world of matter and spirit, cannot fail : in the eternal sense it succeeds if it exists at all ; in the temporal sense, its own truth must one day bring it public recognition. If for the time being the public dignity of thought is lost, we can at least make the gesture of confidence in an ultimate victory. We are not asked, like Admiral Lord Nelson or Captain Makeig Jones, to sacrifice our lives, but only to sacrifice intellectual complacency, prejudice, and personal comfort.

CONTENTS OF VOLS. I—XVII.

VOL. I.

VOL. II.

VOL. III.

VOL. IV.

VOL. V.

VOL. VI.

VOL. VII.

VOL. VIII.

VOL. XI.

VOL. XII.

VOL. XIII.

VOL. XIV.

VOL. XV.

VOL. XVI.